FAKING SMART!

GET HIRED, GET PROMOTED & BECOME A V.P. IN SIX SHORT WEEKS

by

KARL WOLFBROOKS AGER, PhD *(hon.)*
with MARTIN FOSSUM

Illustrations by MATT CORY

*This book is dedicated to
Ella Fossum, Kevin Grange and Mike Marshall.
Thanks also to Katie Basquin, Nathan Everson,
Joe Leich, Jeb Mack, D.P. (wink, wink)
and Miechele Sperling... and the countless others
who put their faith in Faking Smart!*

What Others Have Said About *Faking Smart!*

"Karl W. Ager has done to our understanding of underground business trends what John D. Rockefeller did for dairy science. This book is a tool for anyone interested in learning what it really means to join in today's tumultuous corporate playing field. I should know, I've followed this guy around like a groupie jonesin' for a fix of pure love for many a year."

Clifford Dreidsdale, Chairman
Image Keepers LTD.
Palo Alto, CA

"Once again, Karl W. Ager has done it. He has managed to put together, through a simplified and baffling prolixity, the unique predicament of our social and oligarchic corporatist zeitgeist by means of a perfunctory and liturgical manifesto targeted at dulling reason and sense to pure, abject disavowal."

Beth Veritas,
Wordwatcher Publications
Racine, WI

"Amazing! (Excuse me...) An utter and complete surprise!"

Hans Schmell, Business Editor
Der Berliner Gesundheit!
Essen, Germany

"A must-have for anybody trying to get ahead at work by *Faking Smart!*"

Kevin Sloop, CEO
Career-Getters Inc.
Minot, ND

Contents

	FOREWORD	VI
	INTRODUCTION	VII
	BECOME EMPLOYED!	1
WEEK 1	PIMP YOUR CUBICLE	23
WEEK 2	*WHO MOVED MY CORPORATE LADDER?*	39
WEEK 3	HAIL TO THE CHIEF!	61
WEEK 4	BRING ON THE CLOWNS	81
WEEK 5	ZEN AND THE ART OF *FAKING SMART!*	101
WEEK 6	YOUR PROMOTION TO VP!	115
	AFTERWORD	134

Foreword

THE AIM OF THIS BOOK is to catapult the entry-level employee to the title of VP, in six short weeks. The information in this text, however, may also prove helpful to a more experienced or senior employee wishing to refresh his or her understanding of the basic principles of *Faking Smart!* As a whole, the *Faking Smart! Six-Week Program* is designed to encourage interest in career advancement, provide the reader with the determination to develop and refine individual *Faking Smart!* skill sets, and, most importantly, to help reintroduce and reinforce the motivations that placed the reader on the career parabola in the first place.

We wish to thank everyone who made this book possible. We would be remiss if we did not thank the staff at the FSRI (*Faking Smart!* Research Institute), the countless students and faculty of the FSIHL (the *Faking Smart!* Institute for Higher Learning) and the employees and executives who inhabit the corporate ranks throughout the world. Thanking everyone, however, would be a draining and time-involved task, from which we will refrain. Gratitude is a scarce commodity these days and we would rather bestow it upon ourselves than haphazardly dole it out.

K.W.A. and the FSRI

Introduction

WELCOME AND CONGRATULATIONS! By buying this book you've taken the first step toward achieving a highly successful career as a low-level executive in the ever-expanding world of big business. When you participate in the *Faking Smart! Six-Week Program* you join the millions upon millions who have already achieved corporate success through our program, a program so revolutionary and groundbreaking that it has been dismissed as nonsense, eyewash and malarkey by nearly every expert in the field!

Based loosely on NASA monkey research, Soviet paranormal studies, chaos theory and the lost experimental writings of Thorstein Veblen, the *Faking Smart! Six-Week Program* is one of the most advanced six-week programs of its kind. From the very beginning you'll see that our six-week program is like nothing you could ever imagine. Step by step, our program rockets you through the confusing, yet manageable process of the job hunt, blasts you into the challenging orbit of corporate management and then lands you firmly in the position promised you in the title of this book—*the title of **VP!***

That's right, only six weeks stands between you and the job you should be *dreaming* of having! And when you're *Faking Smart!* you've got nothing to worry about. When you're *Faking Smart!* you *know* that you have the backing of one of the most radical and subversive methods of job-advancement known to mankind. When you're *Faking Smart!* you let us do the thinking for you,

and with only minimal effort and a slight level of motivation you'll soon be able to call your friend and say, *"Hey, guess what? I just became a VP!"*

LAND AN ENTRY-LEVEL JOB—*FAST!*
By following the *Faking Smart!* job-landing strategies, you quickly come to realize that landing an entry-level job is easier than building a peanut butter and jelly sandwich! Right from the start we introduce you to the "do's and don'ts" of the application process, sculpt your image to fit the appropriate business environment and show you how to knock 'em silly with our guaranteed and foolproof interview survival tips. Regardless of your educational background or level of professional experience, our job-landing strategies put you in the back seat while we steer you at breakneck speed toward your corporate destination—*your office cubicle!*

MAKE YOUR CUBICLE YOUR POWER BASE!
Through extensive years of study at the FSRI (*Faking Smart!* Research Institute), we have determined that the cubicle offers the ideal environment for you, the entry-level employee, to achieve our *Faking Smart!* goals. Under the *Faking Smart! Six-Week Program*, from day one your cubicle becomes your power base—a bubble where office communication stops and control over your destiny begins. By following our techniques on cubicle self-management you learn quickly how to hire an assistant, get your operating technologies out of the Stone Age and transform your cubicle from a three-walled fish bowl into an employee fortress where you can begin *Faking Smart!* with comfort and ease!

BECOME A VP IN SIX WEEKS!
That's right. Everything you need to achieve the coveted title of VP is contained right here in this book! The FSRI has done the research, our institute teams have put into practice nearly every stage of the program… all you have to do is sit back and enjoy the ride! Six weeks later, when you emerge as a highly successful, low-level corporate executive, watch your workload plummet, your billable hours sky-rocket and look on as accountability becomes a thing of the past. When you become a VP, you know it! You've got that VP swagger. That's right… you want to become a VP and by purchasing this book you've proved to yourself that you have what it takes! When you're *Faking Smart!* you have nothing left to lose!

Become Employed!

CONGRATULATIONS! By *Faking Smart!* you are taking the first move toward forging a career that you can be happy to tell people about. *How do successful and happy people get the jobs that they have?* They do what you are doing now: they are *Faking Smart!* Six weeks after landing your entry-level job, you will rest easy with the knowledge that you have attained the position of VP at your company—and by definition, being VP is one of the best jobs you can find... *anywhere you work!*

How to Land Your Entry-Level Job

Most entry-level jobs in corporate America involve work with customer service departments, order desks, data entry or in billing. If you are seeking a job in corporate America—*and at this point we hope you are*—the first hurdle you face when looking for an entry-level job is to find a company that has a job opening. Even during periods of economic downturn there are many companies looking for that special person to help them compete in an ever-challenging corporate environment, and in this section of the book *you are that special person!*

This chapter shows you the many ways of discovering companies that are hiring entry-level employees, and below is a list of the most effective methods:

Internet Search

The Internet is a wonderful tool for job searching in our modern business climate. On the web you can access newspaper classifieds, log on to résumé-holding databases such as Monster.com or Google, peruse the listings provided on Craigslist or go directly on to company sites where job-postings are readily available. If weeks and months have gone by, however, and your job search has led you to repeated dead ends, the FSRI recommends that you consider this option: **start your own Internet, job-search company**! It may come as a surprise, but many people who have successfully finished the *Faking Smart! Six-Week Program* obtained employment through starting and building successful companies of their own!

Over time, after your company has grown and is fiscally solid enough to accommodate the full six-week program, the FSRI encourages that you abruptly resign and re-apply as a new entry-level applicant! Applying for entry-level work at your former company puts you head and shoulders above other applicants: your intimate knowledge of the company's inner workings gets you a leg up on your competition and your "cozy" past relationship with the upper brass allows for excellent references and makes you a shoo-in for getting an interview. If you ace the interview and get the job (which you should by following the *Faking Smart! Interview Survival Tips*) you can comfortably begin *Faking Smart!*, Week One, with the raw bulk and enjoyment of the six-week program lying before you like a steaming plate of blueberry waffles!

One thing the FSRI warns against: after your company has gained the sufficient size and market value, don't cut corners and demote yourself straight to VP. If you do this you lose out on the full impact of participating in the six-week program. Sure, you could hire yourself as your own VP, *but you didn't do it by Faking Smart!*

The Cold Call

Calling a company cold (out of the blue) to ask if there is an opening is a terrific way to query companies about job availability. When you have found a company that interests you, go outside (preferably in chilly, winter weather), get out your cell phone and give it a call! After several transfers and disconnections you will eventually wind up talking to somebody who is responsible for hiring for the job you are interested in. You will then be asked to provide your Internet address where an application will be forwarded. Cold calling can be an excellent method of job inquiry. One rule, reminds the FSRI, is to *never leave a message*. Corporate voice boxes are crammed with messages these days, and unless yours is of critical importance it will be ignored and discarded. *"Hook a human being,"* notes the FSRI, *"and let your voice be heard!"*

[If you have more questions about cold calling for a job, call the *Faking Smart!* JOBS HOTLINE for automated service at 1-999-FAKINit. If you want to speak to an operator press "zero," then stay on the line. Later, ask for Cindy at extension #45986, or if not try Rajeev at #344478. Call between 1pm and 4pm GST (Greenland Standard Time)]

The "Temporary" Agency

For many years temporary employment agencies, or temp agents, have become an unlikely mainstay in helping entry-level employees find gainful work. One advantage to temp agencies is that they have the unique ability, through a working knowledge of the corporate employee marketplace, to pair employer with employee. This can be an excellent launch pad for a prospective employee to get his or her name out as someone immediately available for work. The drawback to signing on with temp agencies is that, as their name implies, they aren't around very long. Temp agencies come and go like luck at a roulette table. If you can, apply at a temp agency and insist on getting placement *that very day*. If you don't, you may come back the next day and find that the agency has turned into a take-out teriyaki lunch hut. Such is the reality of this modern method of finding employment. Another thing to remember: if you are fortunate enough to have been placed by a temporary agency, make sure your contract is for no less than *six full weeks*—just enough time for you to make VP!

Networking

Many claim that networking is the best and *only* way of getting an entry-level job. By asking a friend, a neighbor or an old classmate if they know of openings at companies, you quickly expand your circle of inquiry to include this person's entire community of friends and relatives. A better and far more effective way to network, however, is to plumb your list of relations for that **hidden family millionaire!** Yes, *everyone* has a millionaire hidden in the foliage of their family tree, and it is highly likely that this person made his or her millions by running a company that may be interested in hiring you. This might provide just the opportunity for you to get in on the ground level!

When you meet your family millionaire indicate that you are interested in getting into the business *"...for the family's sake."* But be careful not to take just any job thrust at you. If you are asked to sit on the company's corporate board, *turn it down!* If you are offered the position of running a company division or even offered entry as a full VP, decline gracefully. Mention that you want to PROVE yourself and that entry-level work is just the thing to test your mettle. A word of caution: resist the urge to divulge that you are participating in the *Faking Smart! Six-Week Program*. The fact that you are a follower of such a cutting edge job-acceleration program can frazzle the threads of corporate traditionalism that many companies desperately cling to. *"Go in clean,"* advises the FSRI, *"and your chances of making it by Faking Smart! are at their highest!"*

Find a Company You're Interested in and Show Up

Yes! The rumors and urban legends are true! After years of listening to friends telling stories of other friends, the FSRI has concluded, with near certainty, that by simply locating a company and showing up for work you have a high probability of securing employment along-side other entry-level staffers! The hidden truth, discovered the FSRI, is this: **human resource departments and managers loathe the hiring process.** By simply entering a building, finding a cubicle and sitting down to work you are presenting yourself as a company gift. HR doesn't have to verify references, trudge through lengthy cover letters or get reports back on questionable urine samples, and management doesn't have to steal valuable time away from what it does best... *manage!* When you show up and start work—absent the awkward emailing, interviewing and clumsy handshaking—you are telling the company, *"I know the game, and I'm eager to play!"* AND LOOK, YOU'VE ELIMINATED THE APPLICATION AND INTERVIEW

PROCESS IN ONE FELL SWOOP! Sure, you may ruffle a few feathers—nobody likes it when an uninvited guest barges into the party. But just as quickly as this sentiment arises it will vanish. Like stepping out into a street in midtown Manhattan during lunch hour, your presence, initially scorned, will be immediately eclipsed by a mood of acceptance and camaraderie. As everyone knows, business moves fast—too fast for gawkers. When you've shown that you are there (and that you are *there to work*) your job is 99% in the bag!

> [FSRI NOTE: Due to heightened levels of security, some companies require that you wear an ID badge to enter the building or office. In this case, take a 3"x4" piece of clear white paper and print your name under the words: "FSRI Official." Laminate this in plastic, punch a hole in it and hang it by a shoelace around your neck. This should get you past security without hassle. If asked about your ID make it understood that yours is an "official" FSRI ID badge and that they should contact the FSRI offices if they find reason to doubt this. Our operators are standing by to field most of these calls. Remember, never call Karl Wolfbrooks Ager directly… he is rarely in his office and when he is he's usually busy conducting some important meeting or other.]

The Application

Once you have discovered an opening for entry-level work, for many companies it is standard practice for a prospective employee to fill out an application. Some companies, however, require that an applicant not only fill out an application and participate in an interview, but provide a résumé and cover-letter as a supplement. Don't be dismayed. The *Faking Smart!* plan insures that your anxieties will vanish when you use our **easy to follow** guidelines. By streamlining this pre-employment process you are free to devote your attention to more important challenges such as what you will wear during the interview and whether you will go with horn-rimmed or steel-rimmed glasses!

Fill Out Your *Faking Smart!* Application

There are two types of applications you are most likely to receive when applying to a company for work. The first is the "old style" hard copy, and the other, more likely version, is an online application forwarded directly to HR and on to the people looking to fill the position. If it is an old-style application you are submitting, fill it out with a simple ballpoint pen. Do not use a crayon, artist's charcoal pencil, highlighter or Japanese calligraphy brush. When you are finished, hand-deliver or *send* (with adequate postage) the application directly to the appropriate address. With an online format you can enter your information via computer and know, with near certainty, that it will be routed to the mailbox of the person responsible for its evaluation.

Faking Smart! bares its full effects when you are in physical proximity to the environment you are attempting to influence, i.e. the interviewer or employer. The application process is the most difficult in the span of our six-week program in that you are dealing with "unknown" elements that stand between you and your goal... getting the interview *and getting the job*. A well filled out application is essential to your success. Here is an outline for a good *Faking Smart!* application:

Name: (Enter your name here.) Or, if you have a name like Wilberforce, Odjendatwa or Boris this may be the perfect time to visit your local courthouse and sign up for something new. For men, the FSRI recommends first names with real corporate go-getting appeal: names like Chaz, Hugh, and Brock are respected standards. If you are a woman, naming yourself after a tree projects rooted determination and ability to "bend in the wind." First names such as Apple, Willow and Maple have our institution's approval.
Address: (Enter your address here.)
Telephone number: (Enter your telephone number here.)
Email address: (Enter your email address here.)
High school: (Enter your high school here.)
College: (Enter your college or university here.) If you haven't attended a college or university at this point, don't panic. Entry-level work, reports the FSRI, is relatively easy to secure. If, however, you haven't attended an institution of higher learning and you think including a college or university in this section will help your job prospects, choosing one of these *alternative* options may be the path you should take:

OPTION 1

Ivy League schools were created near New York City about a hundred years ago for kids of wealthy families to learn the techniques of socialization and corporate finance. Consequently, having gone to one of these higher tier universities is a cherry atop your ice-cream sundae and nearly guarantees that you'll get your entry-level position. Therefore, take it upon yourself to plan a trip to the East Coast and make a point of visiting Harvard, Yale, Brown or Princeton. Stay at least a few hours in one of these places and then, when you get back home, state on your résumé that you attended one of these institutions with the consolation of having entered a *clear* fact. *You went to Brown.* This is *now* true! If, during your interview, you are probed about your time at your Ivy League school, indicate that you "*sadly, never graduated.*" If needled further for more information or to provide a transcript, burst into tears and say that you didn't last "*even for a year due to pressures and homesickness.*" When your interviewers witness your "sincere" suffering, (that you gave it your best), you've got them on your side of the sympathy gambit and you'll probably be asked to start the very next day!

OPTION 2

Hire a qualified hypnotist to implant artificial memories of **"your four, wonderful years at Yale!"** This may take quite a while, but when your reprogramming is complete, you should have no apprehension about including Yale as your alma mater.  Be sure to have your hypnotist implant a bad memory or two—a failed class, *ughh!*, or a cheating girlfriend—this will help to strengthen your claim during the interview and help make your new "old" memories more vivid and convincing!

When you have finished with the interview process and have the job, go back to your hypnotist and have your *real* memory restored. Then schedule additional sessions that will erase the memory of *all* your previous hypnosis sessions. When you've done this you can say that you've safely skirted any ethical concerns regarding honesty and you can start the six-week program with a clean conscience!

OPTION 3

If you are of college age and have had fairly good grades you might want to actually consider entering an Ivy League school. After you receive your diploma from one of these schools, take the next two or three years to pad your work history with related career employment. Then, when you feel you've made enough progress fill out an application for a job and pick up the *Faking Smart! Six-Week Program* from the beginning. **(This option is clearly the most time-consuming of the four listed. In a pinch, "Take the route of least resistance," insists the FSRI, "and stick with options 1, 2 or 4!")**

OPTION 4

Go to any institute of higher learning and get a diploma. It doesn't really matter where you go. A community college. A state school. Chances are… if you've gone to one of these places of higher learning you will be a strong candidate for the entry-level position you are applying for! You may even decide that the FSIHL (the *Faking Smart!* Institute for Higher Learning) is a place where you might thrive and excel! At the FSIHL we offer a fully accredited four-week Bachelor of Arts degree in *Faking Smart!* [Again, be discreet when putting the FSIHL in your college education field. Having an elite degree from the FSIHL may be seen as an overt challenge to the status quo and you may be passed right by. Use judgment when disclosing the fact that you attended such an exclusive, land-shaking institution!]

Employment History: There are two approaches to filling out this sometimes intimidating section of your application. The First: if you have experience in corporate office work… by all means put it down. Showing that you know how to conduct yourself professionally in a corporate environment is excellent help in securing your employment at a new firm. Second: if you don't have experience in entry-level corporate work, try to think of things you've done in the past that made money. (Poker games, car theft or drug dealing should be excluded from your list.) Be honest, *but creative!* If you worked as a cheese curd server at the Minnesota State Fair in the summer of 2010, indicate that you were a "Dairy Logistics Analyst" for the

State of Minnesota in 2010. If you worked as a cashier at a gas station for a few months just out of high school, mark down that you were a *Petroleum Industries Retail Consultant*. The more official your job title sounds the better you look! The truth is, though, your prospective employer wants to know one basic thing: *is this person going to show up on Monday?* If you can convince your interviewer that there is a good chance that you will... *you'll probably get the job!*

The Résumé

It is generally perceived that the résumé is nothing more than a single sheet of paper providing clear and concise information of one's academic achievements and work history. However true, in most circumstances, there are some who take the résumé to a different level... those who see it as a biographical canvass; a way of transforming this rusty tool of business traditionalism to a demonstration of high art by using this medium as a *"mirror to one's soul."* There have been instances of applicants investing in expensive European parchments to serve as a background for their personal information. Others have gone to such lengths as to emboss their beloved résumés in gold leaf. There is even one account of an entry-level applicant who took the entire population of his small town in rural Missouri and had them spell out his résumé on the high school football field. Using aerial photography he enlarged the picture and had it mounted on a billboard opposite the offices of the firm he was applying to in New York City. Did he get the job? *Who cares?* What we *have* found at the FSRI, however, is that more often then not, our method provides the clearest results, and with minimal effort you can produce the best résumé statistically possible!

Create Your *Faking Smart!* Résumé

With regards to personal and educational information, the résumé and application are nearly identical in nature. What separates the résumé from the application is the degree of description required for each category.

When creating a résumé it is necessary to include a line or two of additional information under each sub-heading. If, for example, you included *Lawn Mowing* under "Work Experience" in your application, for the résumé follow this up with description of your duties as a lawn mower. For example:

Lawn Mower: Responsible for trimming grass to client-specified height. Managed clipping removal and relocation. Beautified areas around stone walkway with grass trimmer. Sometimes took out garbage.

By including a more detailed explanation of what you did as a lawn mower you make a better impression of what your job responsibilities actually were. You bring your old job to life!

One obvious difference between the résumé and the application are the résumé's "Objective" and "Professional Activities" fields. Whereas, in the application, it is clear that you are "applying" for something, in the résumé *you* have to make it clear. The "Objective" field should contain one full sentence indicating your intentions at the company you are applying to. If you are applying at IBM, for example, your sentence may be similar to this one: "To apply for an entry-level, cubicle position at IBM." This is an example of a short and accurate statement. What you don't want to do is write the following: "To apply for an entry-level, cubicle position at IBM while utilizing the *Faking Smart! Six-Week Program.*" This will likely harm your prospects at this company. Remember: *never* identify yourself as a practitioner of *Faking Smart!* techniques or you will be quickly removed from consideration!

As for the "Professional Activities" field, this section is here to indicate what work or activities you've participated in *beyond* what was expected of you at your previous occupations. Including volunteer work here is especially effective in drawing an employer's attention. If you saved whales one summer during high school, this might be an excellent activity to mention. *Everyone loves a whale!* Ever plant a tree? State that you have! When you show that you have other interests you portray yourself as a "rounded" individual... *and someone likely to be brought on board!*

The Cover Letter

> *"If the résumé is the cake you are handing over to your future employer, the cover letter is the platter it's served on."*
> Karl W. Ager, 2009

While focus on the cover letter has been blurred by all the attention the résumé has received in recent years, it still should be seen, in its own right, as playing at least a supporting role in the application process. While on the surface, this letter might seem to be nothing more than a thin wrapping for the real package inside (your resume), the cover letter can also be a place where small mistakes can sound the death knell for your chances at getting an interview.

Our research foundation has done close to a million studies on the question of the cover letter and the results are conclusive. There is *one* way to write an effective cover letter. Here it is:

Name
Address
Phone number
Email address

The Whateveritis Company

To whomever it may be of concern:

I am inscribing this letter to indicate my will and testament to apply for entry-level stature at _____.

As a skilled and able executor of trades, I have grave confidence that I am the most suited and upstanding candidate for the post. I have had the happenstance to prove myself in many such-and-so-forth a task. Given the grace of your generous bestowance, I will work profusely to make good, that a job is a job well done at _____.

Lastly, others have born witness to my cut and trim, now let me show _____ from what grade of salt my character is mined.

> **Without question, you will find my experience more than ample to fulfill the responsibilities as an entry-level lackey at _____. Again, thank you for taking the time to peruse my application and I look forward to our future tête á tête!**
>
> **Most amicably and sincerely,**
>
> _____

The fatal flaw in a typical cover letter, our research institute has found, is a disorganized or sloppy presentation. The letter should be short and to the point, punctuated accordingly and courtly in word use. If, in the course of applying for entry-level jobs, you still haven't managed to land an interview, keep on trying. To some extent, the application process is a numbers game: the more applications you send out, the more likely you are to get an interview. Some of our students at the FSIHL have resorted to throwing multiple application packages at the same company (under differing names and addresses) until one of them stuck. Which cover letter format was used in those successful applications? The answer: ***a near carbon copy of the example given above!***

The Interview

Congratulations! So you've got your application in and they've called you or messaged you to set up an interview. After all that hard work you are actually going to sit face to face with another human being and prove that you are the candidate the company is looking for. It might seem that from this point on the rest of the work is going to be easy. Well, that's where you are right! Yes, by following the *Faking Smart!* plan for this phase of the *Faking Smart! Six-Week Program*, getting the job is easy, and the cards, you will see, are stacked in your favor. But preparation is essential—stick to what we know and you are guaranteed a smooth ride straight up to the velvet carpet that leads to your new cubicle!

Set Up the Interview

At some point, after one of your applications or résumés makes the cut, a company representative will contact you to set up an interview. Allow this person to set the date and time and then see if it fits in with your schedule. If you have more than one company calling to set up interviews, be sure that you don't schedule these interviews close together. If, for example, you've scheduled two interviews in a day—one in Chicago and one in San Diego—chances are, due to geographical distance, this will be a hard promise to keep. When speaking with the interviewer, try to sound as professional as possible. Don't giggle and moan over the phone. Be polite and courteous. If they ask if 2:30 on Thursday, March 14th is okay, respond by clarifying whether or not they meant 2:30 a.m. or 2:30 p.m.? Asking this question shows that you are *detail-oriented*. Lastly, it is sometimes appropriate to request reimbursement for your travel expenses. Be *sure* to confirm that this is within company policy. Asking a company for compensation for an entry-level interview is generally considered in poor taste.

As the date for your interview draws close there are a three things you must do before walking through those office doors: first, you must learn what it is, exactly, the company you are interviewing for does; second, based on what your research revealed, select appropriate attire or business uniform; and third, augment your image with several of our "sure to impress" *Faking Smart! Interview Survival Tips*.

Just What Does This Company Do?

So you are scratching your head. *"Okay,"* you say to yourself. *"I've got the interview. Now, just what does InCredidata (or whatever company it is) do?"* The first thing you should do is some footwork (or browser-work) and discover everything you can about the company that you are seeking employment with. Try your Facebook or Twitter buds right off the bat. Let all your friends know that you have an interview at InCredidata (or whatever company it is) and see what kind of reaction you get. Were the responses positive? Has anyone ever worked at InCredidata or does anyone work there now? What was it like? This should provide a snapshot of what it might feel like to wake up every morning, shower, feed your French Bulldog and head to your InCredidata office for a full day of work.

If the complaints run high, don't let this discourage you... *everyone* wants to grunt and grumble about their job!

Next, do an Internet search and hunt through archival indexes of InCredidata in the news. Is the company known for its trendy and hip ad campaigns? Does InCredidata have subsidiaries in fashion or retail? Does it sponsor any college bowl games? This type of research will help you to get a sense of InCredidata's larger corporate profile. After you've done this go directly to the corporate website and see what you find. Are there pictures of employees on this site? How are they dressed? Look up the list of company VPs. Are they an attractive and energetic-looking staff? Are their names simple and easy to remember? Can you find a picture of the CEO and get an idea of whether or not this is a person you can relate to? Is this CEO somebody who seems to be in control and someone who projects the kind of good corporate image that immediately gains your trust? If you've answered yes to any of these questions it is probably an excellent company in which to implement your use of the *Faking Smart! Six-Week Program!*

Now you have prepared for the interview. You have first-hand accounts, through soliciting stories from your friends, of what it is like to work at InCredidata. You have an understanding of what InCredidata's corporate image is and what events or sports it sponsors. Lastly, you've got a glimpse into the soul of the company by seeing how its employees dress and by looking into the eyes of its CEO! It's that easy. Armed with your thorough preparation there should be no curveballs the interviewers can possibly throw. With a solid understanding of what InCredidata (or whatever the company you are applying for) is all about, you stand an excellent chance of getting the job!

"Oh, Gosh! What Do I Wear?"

Don't panic. The FSRI has come up with four basic attire plans that will get you through this seemingly tough decision.

In the years that the FSRI has been studying market-place attire we have developed a great advantage in helping you put on what you need to make your interview a knockout success. It is an axiom in the business world that looking your best means working at your best, so picking an image that works becomes a critical element to getting the job. The four basic looks are listed below:

1. The anti-corporate look. Since the dawn of the industrial age, the anti-corporate look has become a must for anybody wanting to get ahead in today's business world. While this look projects an attitude of indifference—cultural revulsion (*check out those body-piercings!*) and lack of concern for corporate people or anything to do with corporate America—at the same time it has the underlying effect of creating the perception of a hidden self-confidence and even latent genius. While the anti-corporatist comes off as  laid back and more interested in skating, snowboarding or riding motorcycles than going to work, the unseen message says **"Hey, get off my back, or I might quit and start my own company!"**

The anti-corporate look, when considering the above, seems ideal for someone trying to get ahead at a company by *Faking Smart!* This look, however, carries with it certain pitfalls. At bigger companies and multi-conglomerates the anti-corporate look can have the negative effect of coming off as self-serving and even "counter-corporate." Unfortunately, this is true. Remember, the bigger a company is, the less they want an anti-corporatist around. It is distracting (all that skateboard noise going up and down the halls) and may inspire a sense of individualism and self-determination among the rank-and-file; something no corporation would tolerate under most circumstances.

2. The business-formal look. A company that requires business-formal wear wants to project what those stiff black suits are saying: *"We mean business."* Companies of this nature are usually financial firms (banks, Wall Street brokers, hedge funds, accountancies and insurance companies), high-end service companies like upper-class hotels, restaurants and funeral parlors, and movie house ushers. The circumstances where you might find it necessary to go business-formal are, obviously, few and far between, given that cubicle-based work is your focus... nonetheless, there may be instances where this look warrants application. Business formal represents a stuffiness associated with conventionality and predictability. Someone wearing this outfit is looking to convey a sense of security and conservatism and to operate with a sort of Old World snootiness while shoulder-to-shoulder with workplace colleagues. No jokes are said when wearing these dandy threads, unless implied with innuendo or whispered discretely in bathroom stalls or behind closed doors. Once outside the office, freed from the shackles of corporate stodginess, this suit comes alive! Watch it while it rants and raves over happy-hour margaritas! Observe its cunning after a gin-and-tonic has loosened its tongue and sent it into lascivious laughter! Yes, this suit *means business... but business of what kind?*

Many entry-level employees get into a trap when they incorporate the business-formal look during an interview. Some get it into their heads that wearing such a "nice suit" will earn them points during this important meeting. This, however, is wrong. If you aren't applying to one of the types of business-formal firms mentioned above you might unwittingly embarrass yourself. Use the business formal attire only in the most serious of situations.

3. Corporate-casual, the lifeblood of corporate attire. The cultural revolution of the '60s brought with it drugs, free sex and a skepticism when it came to trusting the government... but it also came with benefits, such as the loosening of attitudes regarding what was acceptable workplace attire. The corporate-casual look finally made the workplace more accessible to those that couldn't pretend to afford playing the business-formal game. Today, according to the FSRI's recent research on corporate attire, 91.63% of corporations in the U.S. follow a corporate-casual code of dress. It allows for a level of intellectual freedom and creativity and is by far the method of attire most should study and implement.

A tip on what passes for corporate-casual: anything that basically looks nice. No holes in jeans... and no jeans for that matter. Shirts are clean, but not necessarily pressed. Socks are laundered and underwear fresh and minty in odor. Men, if you are daring and have one, try throwing on a tie under your sweater. Women, modest cleavage is good—midriffs (muffin-tops)... sorry, but no.

Corporate-casual is most likely the mode of attire you should choose to wear during your interview. Going corporate-casual makes you look... *corporate!*

4. The collegiate-upstart look. The collegiate-upstart look is reserved for those in their mid-twenties who have recently graduated from college. If you are applying to a company that is said to have many recent grads as hires, this might be your best choice of attire. The look expresses an innocence and openness—a projection of deference, loyalty and sacrifice; the kind of relationship expected by a company that takes you under its wing as the newest *"member of the family."*

The essence of the collegiate-upstart look manifests itself in the emulation of a kind of schoolyard charm. For boys, a striped alumnus tie might be in order, overlaid by a sport jacket with embroidered fraternity crest. Girls... knee-high pleated skirts and knee-high socks project the epitome of a collegiate look; this with a light, argyle V-neck sweater makes for an ideal ensemble. Remember, when wearing the collegiate-upstart look, you are young and energetic. You are the "yes" person! If you are asked to bury a corpse in the field behind the building, your response is *"Where is the shovel?"* If asked to work overtime for no pay, you say, *"Toss me one of those energy drinks and I'm on it!"*

A note of caution: If you are older than 45 pulling off the collegiate-upstart look might become increasingly tricky. If, say, you are 58 and you bound into the interview with a school-crested jacket and chinos there is a likelihood that you may be deemed an oddity, and after a brief interview you might find yourself getting the *"don't call us, we'll call you"* line. If in doubt, go corporate-casual. Corporate-casual is, as argued by the FSRI, the best bet when one is confronted with an interview. It allows attention to be drawn away from you and placed in directions where *Faking Smart!* is in control!

So there you have it. Secure in the knowledge that you are wearing the right outfit, your confidence grows and your chance of success grows with it!

Faking Smart! Interview Survival Tips

The FSRI has discovered several tips that will increase your chances of pulling off a successful interview. The results of our research suggest that the more tips you observe and utilize from the list below, the better your odds are of getting the job! Our research institute has completed the studies, your task is to make them work for you. Good luck!

1. **Glasses make you look 63% smarter.** For several years now the FSRI Optical Effects Department has pursued an on-going study on the relevance of eyewear at the interview and during your job. Our conclusive results have shown that wearing glasses makes you look an incredible 63% smarter. Look at the evidence in these pictures:

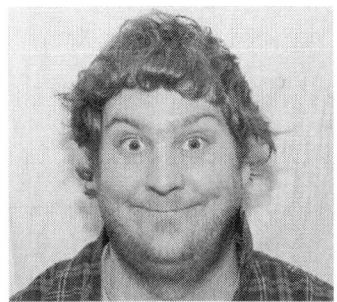
Before.

After!

2. **Carrying a cell phone and laptop with you at all times make you appear 28% more professional.** Technology is a critical element on today's business environment. Showing that you are up-to-date with the latest technical innovations gives you the edge up on your competition! A reminder: make sure to power up your new piece of technology before impressing someone with it.

3. **iPods, though a trendy, tech-savvy gadget, should not be used during interviews.** You may wish to be listening to Justin Bieber's latest single more than the gibberish drooling from your interviewer's mouth, but plugging into an iPod during an interview implies that you are someone with an attention problem, and this may discourage your interviewers from giving you the job. We suggest you eliminate the iPod, or any Mp3 player for that matter, from daily life.

4. **No pets—leave your hamsters and cats at home.** While it might seem like fun to have Tolstoy, your four-month-old tabby, leap out from the pocket

of your suit coat in the middle of the interview... projecting yourself as a "pet person" may stand in the way of your receiving full approval from your interviewers. "*Leave 'em at home,*" proclaims the FSRI, "*and fiddle with your furry beasts in private!*"

5. No hardhats or welding masks–heads should be clean and bare. Although these pieces of head and eye protection are standard safety protocol at some workplaces, remember one thing: *you're applying for office work!* Your daily health concerns at InCredidata (or whatever company you are interviewing for) are not eye damage or risk of burns—they involve things like lower back pain and ear infections from bacteria-laden headsets. Leave your construction equipment at home... your head bare and barbered, your hands clean and lotion-soft!

6. No nose rings that weigh more than 8 ounces. The desire your interviewers may have to tug at your statement of non-conformity should preclude your desire to wear your largest of nasal rings. This type of interaction—between interviewer and interviewee—is deeply discouraged by the FSRI.

7. No facial tattoos. Unless you can claim lineage to one of the tribes of the South Pacific, keep your face free of ink.

8. No goatees (men)–that was so nineties. With the rapid development of facial hair arrangement there has been a revision in what beard trim is deemed cool. The goatee no longer falls in that category. Men... **shave it off and go with the Abe Lincoln beard or the handlebar mustache.** (At the time of this book's publication, this was the official recommendation of the FSRI. As is often the case, fashion trends evolve quickly and without much warning. Perhaps the goatee will, once again, rise to prominence. If, in the future, this happens to be the case, the FSRI will *still* insist that the goatee is to be an avoided method of facial hair presentation.)

9. No Twittering during the interview.

10. No Tai Chi while waiting in the lobby.

11. No throwing up during the interview—only before and after.

12. No smoking during the interview.

13. No smoking a pipe during the interview.

14. NEVER smoke marijuana unless you are given permission by a parent or legal guardian.

15. NEVER come to an interview drunk or heavily sedated—wait till you have the job to see what is permissible.

The Interview

After all the preparation you've made prior to this interview, *finally* you have the opportunity to meet your prospective employer face to face! Supported by the vast knowledge of the FSRI there is nothing you need to get nervous or be worried about. *Faking Smart!* is behind you all the way. Just take a deep breath and enter that interview room!

In all likelihood you already have the job. Your *Faking Smart!* application, cover letter and résumé have given you a solid foundation for presenting yourself as a corporate go-getter. You know everything there is to know about the reputation of the company interviewing you by the thorough Internet research you've conducted. You've chosen an appropriate corporate apparel style (by following the FSRI's advice on business attire), and you've studied and rehearsed the surefire *Faking Smart! Interview Survival Tips*. You've got everything going for you, so take it easy and bask in the warmth of being a player in this revolutionary job-building plan! *The Faking Smart! Six-Week Program* has got your back!

While waiting in the lobby for your name to be called, sit still and avoid yawning or crying. Batting at a fly with the copy of the *Wall Street Journal* downloaded to your Kindle is sure to gain you some corporate street cred. If there is someone else waiting with you this may be the perfect time to bring up the "profit windfall" you plan to make in Indo-Chinese housing derivatives. Projecting the image of being a savvy real estate investor is a great way to start making new friends! Then, when your interviewer(s) come out to meet you, be sure to follow these *two rules of behavior* to help you complete your *Faking Smart!* impression!

1. **Show that you are in control.** If you are a male shaking a male interviewer's

hand, grab it firmly and then quickly draw his hand toward your heart. Then wrap your other arm around his neck and growl in a playful way. If you are a male shaking a female interviewer's hand, bow delicately and avoid eye contact at all cost. Women, curtsy politely and then offer your hand to be kissed by a male interviewer. If you are a woman confronting another woman interviewer, however, extend a hand, then, once your hand is taken press your fingernails deeply into her palm and clench your teeth while hissing the words, "*It's a pleasure to meet you.*"

2. Act engaged. When your interviewers ask why you want to work at their firm, don't whistle and check your phone for text messages. Give a simple reply: *"For the same reasons you work here!"* Then explain your passion for corporate employment and your excitement in starting your career here at InCredidata (or whatever company it is). Ask for your interviewer's names and jot them down on a notepad so that when the meeting is over you can say, *"Hey, Jim, thanks for taking the time to bring me here. You have a great company and I'd like to be a part of it."* Or tell the other interviewer, *"You brought up some nice points, Tiffany, and I hope you find me as someone who could be a team player here at InCredidata (or whatever company it is)."* After you've answered their questions and the interview comes to a close, *"Go bold,"* says the FSRI, *"and ask if it's possible to see your cubicle that very day!"*

Yes! It's all that easy! By *Faking Smart!* you've made the right impression! While leaving, wink at an attractive office worker as you pull out your phone and jog toward the elevator. Banter about last night's game with some of "the guys" you see hanging around the coffee stand. You guessed it, for *six full weeks* you will consider this place your home! Expect the call the next day—noonish—and then get ready to start the grit and grind of the next phase of the *Faking Smart! Six-Week Program!*

Accepting the Job Offer

Congratulations. You did it! When they call to tell you that you have the job, sound excited. *This is very important!* Tell them you are happy to hear that you've been accepted at InCredidata (or whatever company it is) and that you are eager to start!

There are now a number of things you need to do before moving on to the next stage of the six-week program. Be sure that you agree with your new employer to start work on a Monday *(this is crucial in regards to the scheduling we have outlined for the following week.)* The second thing you need to consider is that, if you don't live in the same town where you have been offered your new job, you will need to move in proximity to the office building where you will soon be working. (This helps to make for a manageable commute.) If you have to move, pack enough food and clothing for six weeks and then find a place to live. If you already live near your place of employment, you have avoided a serious amount of stress and hassle. *And, yes, your friends will love you because of it!*

Now, get ready to start Week One of the *Faking Smart! Six-Week Program!* You may feel like this is a time to kick back and take it easy for a few days… *you landed the job, didn't you?* But this is far from the case. Week One of the six-week program offers some of the most challenging aspects of the full *Faking Smart!* program. Preparing yourself mentally, at least a little bit, will go a long way in making Week One a success. Try yoga… or pick up an instrument and join a brass band if you have a set of sturdy lips. Poisonous snake charming, bungee-jumping, skydiving and ice-climbing are all encouraged by the FSRI!

Again… good luck! You've been *Faking Smart!* and it's paid off. By doing what we think you should be doing, you are miles ahead of your fellow entry-level employees. "*Faking Smart!,*" boasts the FSRI, "*is a way to get where you want, when you want and how we want you to arrive at your ultimate corporate destiny!*"

Week 1
PIMP YOUR CUBICLE

CONGRATULATIONS! You've landed your entry-level job! Now the **power of promotion** lies in your hands. By carefully following the techniques we provide for you, in no time at all you'll be calling your family or friend to say, *"Guess what, I'm a VP, and it only took me six weeks to do it!"* By landing a job you've demonstrated to yourself that you have everything it takes to succeed. With a moderate level of motivation and a small amount of work you will see that the shortcut to your dream is only six weeks away!

Day One: You and Your Workplace

Before you show up to work on Monday there are a number of things you must bring with you to make a guaranteed *Faking Smart!* first impression:

1. A 4"x 6" picture of a really attractive person (this is your "significant other"), framed and in a holder or stand.
2. A TOSS Pyramid. (Visit our website for information on the TOSS Pyramid.)
3. A copy of Karl W. Ager's *Doing Business, Harvard Style*.
4. A copy of Karl W. Ager's *Thinking Outside the Cube—Conducting Your On-Line Business While at Work*.

The chances of you having an attractive significant other are slim, so we advise that you obtain a picture of someone else, perhaps a cousin or a neighbor. We also provide free images for download of people we consider attractive on our website, www.fakingsmart.com. The other items, such as the TOSS Pyramid and book jackets, can be obtained at the same website for a minimal price. Since the books mentioned above have yet to find premium publisher representation, only the jackets are now available, *but don't worry, these can be wrapped around a cheap, used book for equal effect!*

Meet the Boss

So, it's your first day and you've arrived right on time, steaming coffee in hand. The lobby is calming and the receptionist friendly as he or she directs you to the room where you are to meet with your manager for the morning powwow. It is most likely that you will be training with other new hires, so don't be surprised if you aren't alone.

Reach out and smile as you shake hands with your new boss and mention how nice she looks. Be polite and offer her a sip from your latte and then find out where the employee break room is and when you eat lunch. Your boss will then get things rolling by requesting that each new hire begin by introducing him or herself. When she comes to you, stand up and recite your name correctly and in full. When this icebreaker is over she'll have everyone follow her for a brief tour of the building. This will provide an excellent opportunity for you to inquire about emergency exits, whether the building has been earthquake retro-fitted and what company procedure is with respect to global warming and African killer-bee evacuations. "*Safety comes first,*" is something you might offer with enthusiasm during the tour. This is a great way to show your boss and the other new hires that you are concerned about the environment *and* your own safety… because showing concern for your own safety is an indication of your concern for everyone's safety!

After your building tour, you will most likely be shown to the central operating floor where an array of beautiful cubicles will stretch out before you. This is where all the action of your company takes place! Phones ring, cubicles chatter with the rhythmic tat-tat-tat of fingers striking keyboards and hands shoot upwards for supervisor help like those of schoolchildren fawning for a teacher's attention. This is the nerve center of the company where careers are made and broken and this is where you begin the first stages of the *Faking Smart! Six-Week Program!*

This is also where you make your first assertive move!

While hours of training and new hire protocol stand between you and being assigned your own cubicle, take the initiative and find a cubicle right now! Ask to be excused for a moment, then eye the rows of cubicles for available space. Locate, if you can, the most isolated cubicle and grab it. Get out the picture of your significant other and place it on the desk. Then get out your books and lean them up in a corner. Finally, pull out your TOSS Pyramid and give it a roll.

Congratulations! You've just staked a claim on your first cubicle in the *Faking Smart! Six-Week Program*! By taking charge and picking out your cubicle you are telling your boss and everyone else, *"Hey, I'm here! Let's get busy."* When others walk by your cubicle, they'll be awestruck: you've got a hot boyfriend or girlfriend, you're a motivated self-improver and reader of smart, cutting-edge business books and you convey that you have revolutionary management know-how by your admiration and respect (and future implementation, of course) of the powers of the TOSS Pyramid and the *TOSS Executive Decision-Making System*. Your boss will nod with approval and the rumors will spread quickly that there's a new hotshot on the floor—*and it all happens during your first hour on the job!*

You're making your first moves in *Faking Smart!* Now brave your way through the morning training session and at lunch tell your boss that you're taking the rest of the day off to meet with your old friend Samantha Connors (one of the names of the VPs you found during your Internet research on company personnel). The second part of a new hire's first day is typically wasted filling out forms, practicing simulation exercises and role-playing and you've got way more serious things to be thinking about ahead in Day Two.

Day Two: Create a Cubicle that Works

One of the most exciting moments in the *Faking Smart! Six-Week Program* is when an old cubicle is transformed into a monument to personal projection—a place to serve as headquarters and home for the nine days it takes to implement this portion of our *Faking Smart! Six-Week Program*. That the cubicle has been long neglected as a base for employee empowerment is indication of the sorrowful state business is in today, but by taking charge, you and your cubicle will become an inseparable platform marking a noticeable shift in your office presence.

While a total-cubicle remodel is at once exciting and fun, it is very important that the basic functions of the cubicle remain intact. In the years that our research foundation has been studying the effects of the remodeled cubicle, the lesson learned again and again was to keep the cubicle operational to the extent that is still offers the employee the ability to perform his or her essential job requirements. If you go too far with pimping your cubicle and fail to keep this in mind you may quickly build up frustration that you aren't able to fulfill your work responsibilities. In other words, you might end up with an exceptionally rad cubicle, but, in the worst case, no job with which to enjoy it! Avoiding this disaster is paramount to succeeding in the first stages of our program, and following the advice we give will help you avoid any unnecessary hardship.

The Makeover Basics

You can do just about anything your imagination allows when designing your new cubicle, but research at the FSRI has determined that there are three aspects that must be addressed to insure your cubicle make-over is a success. The three things necessary are to replace your existing chair, update your old company computer to a new model and install a tested and approved CCCU (Cubicle Climate Control Unit).

The first aspect to address is the replacement of your existing chair. Several studies at our foundation have shown that the typical cubicle chair is one of the most dangerous health hazards to modern business employees. Anecdotal research at our institute has come to the stunning conclusion that a standard-issue cubicle chair can render a user paralyzed in an average of 8.6 months (give or take two-to-45 years). Throwing out this instrument of torture is essential to preserving your health and longevity and to creating a comfortable cubicle environment. Therefore, we suggest you replace your old chair with an upper-end executive's model, preferably of leather with padded armrests and a high back. *"If you aren't healthy, comfortable and relaxed at work,"* states the FSRI, *"why work at all?"* Most big box office retailers have a wide selection of executive chairs and can deliver straight to your workplace!

The second thing that must be done is to get rid of your Jurassic computer system and replace it with a lightning fast, new-gen set-up. The computers employers issue to new hires, our foundation has discovered, are most likely out-of-date, recycled, 10- to 15-year-old, former state accounting hulks. Updating from one of these dinosaurs will improve your eyesight, relieve symptoms of carpal tunnel syndrome, eliminate hearing loss and slow facial wrinkling.

Along with your new computer system you will need to subscribe to

DSL or broadband service to facilitate online connectivity. In an effort to instill discipline among the ranks, many entry-level employees are given limited use of, or even *denied* access to the Internet. Getting wired is your way of leaping over this institutional barrier so that you can surf the net for sports scores, update your Facebook or Twitter accounts and participate in the lively art of office e-memoing **WITHOUT RUNNING UP YOUR BILL USING YOUR SMART PHONE OR OTHER WIRELESS DEVICE.** Calling any of your local Internet providers will yield results. Simply request online service over the phone and indicate your address, floor and floor-plan map, cubical number and billing information and they will be eager to serve. (You might want to schedule this hookup process while your boss is at lunch.) Remember, your boss most likely has a limited knowledge of technology—*that's why she became a manager and not an IT specialist.* Consequently, a few lines of techno-babble and your justification for these updates will quickly be given the green light. Secondly, you've already proved yourself to be an office maverick... chances are the rest of the floor is looking to *you* to set the new benchmark for cubicle survival. You're the cool one on the floor now—a good manager will see this and give you the room you need to operate.

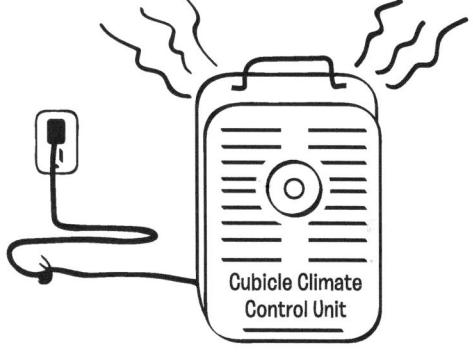
Cubicle Climate Control Unit

Finally, the simple step of incorporating a state of the art CCCU will help you feel comfortable while doing your work. Many offices today chill their cubicle floors to a frightening 58 degrees Fahrenheit, and obtaining a CCCU will help your cubicle environment considerably, allowing you the ability to catch a few critically needed "zzz's" when desired. (Remember to only purchase a CCCU with the "*FSRI Seal of Approval.*")

Budgeting

You will most likely require the help of an outside contractor to assist you with the things that need to be done on your second day of work. You may also need to negotiate financial assistance to be able to pay for the remodeling of your cubicle and you might want to consider applying to a number of credit card companies to help you through this part of the program. Many of the big box home-remodeling and office-maximizing stores still have various *"buy now, pay later"* plans that allow you to defer payment for as much as a year after your purchase. Whatever the outcome, don't worry about over-spending, in less than six weeks you'll be operating on VP salary scale and all this will be easily affordable when you transfer the balance to your company expense account.

In a worst case scenario, when you are in a bad credit situation and find yourself unable to secure a short-term loan, www.fakingsmart.com offers intermittent cubicle-pimping scholarships and sweepstakes! So, check our website for current contest information. Otherwise, a little bit of creativity and help from someone with a set of carpentry tools can get you where we want you to be.

Pimpin' With Style!

So you've got the basics down; your new chair, new computer setup and CCCU have dragged your workspace out of the stone age and into the 21st century. Now let loose and allow your cubicle to express the inner you! With the right setup your workspace is transformed from cubicle to *office fortress*, an impregnable base from which you can comfortably and privately pursue the next phase of your *Faking Smart! Six Week Program*.

SOME OF THE CUBICLE PIMPING STYLES APPROVED BY THE FOUNDATION:

1. **Far Eastern, Zen motif.** What could be more calming than a rock garden and a Zen water fountain?
2. **Pimpin' in da Hood.** Complete with sub-woofers, rear-view mirror and fuzzy dice!
3. **Messy Genius.** This works well for those on a low budget… most of the paper overflow can be obtained in recycling bins near the dumpsters in office parking lots.
4. **Neat Freak.** Inspired by Northern German Functionalism.
5. **Country-Clubber.** Please, no low-end, used clubs…
6. **The Huntsman.** Firearms are illegal for public exhibit in most municipalities, so review local statutes before hanging a rifle on your back wall.

7. **The Environmentalist.** Everyone loves office plants!
8. **South Beach Sunshine.** Nothing feels better than sand between the toes while you answer customer complaints!
9. **New York Hipster.** Exploring your "artistic" side has been proven to increase productivity.
10. **Oval Office.** "The Buck Stops Here," reads your authoritative and brassy placard. This classy cubicle style is only for those who are bold and want to intimidate right off the bat!

In the years that we have been doing our research, these were some of the most effective themes for cubicle pimping. Remember, regardless of the style you choose to go with, there will be a certain level of surprise generated in your office when your crew comes in to do their work. Some of your co-workers may express jealousy over your project; others may even describe the excitement of whirring table saws and snapping nail guns as a disturbance, but the end result of the short time it will take to transform your work environment from one of oppressiveness to one of comfortable productivity will benefit you in the long run.

Hopefully, within a few short hours, your cubicle is pimped. Now take a long break and come back and enjoy the rest of the day. *You just might be able to get some real work in by quittin' time.* But don't worry, like the first week of college, (for those of you who have served time there), the expectations for a new hire's first week are low and you might find this a good opportunity to prepare for your third day at work. Get online and learn about your state prison system's work-release programs and your local high-schools with robust foreign-exchange student populations. This is excellent preparation for next the step in the your first week on the job—*obtaining an assistant!*

Day Three: Hire an Assistant

How do real-world VPs become as successful as they are? The answer is simple: they have had the good fortune of acquiring a loyal and skilled assistant to do most of the heavy lifting that their job requires. In today's hurried and tumultuous business environment there is no way a VP could handle all that is demanded of him or her without the help and guidance of an executive assistant. It is simply impossible. All executive-level employees hold this knowledge sacred. It is therefore essential, in this stage of the

Faking Smart! Six Week Program, that you acquire your own assistant and quickly learn the benefits of this invaluable relationship.

Call in Sick

Because of the demands that hiring an assistant will place on your time during this, your third day at work, calling in sick offers the perfect solution. Without knowing much about your medical history, your boss will most likely trust you enough to believe any excuse you may give her for your inability to complete the day's work responsibilities. You might mention how a minor bout with scurvy has left you lethargic and in pain. You might also claim to have a recurring botfly infection and give her your assurances that you will be back in full force the next day. Whatever the case, establishing an early and consistent struggle with bewildering health irregularities is sure to gain you the leeway you'll need when you find yourself tight for time and discover your work schedule getting in the way of your next *Faking Smart!* advancement tactic.

Day three, for that matter, should be your first use of a sick excuse. Leave a message the night before, by email or by calling company voicemail, that you've just been diagnosed with a case of scurvy; then call again early in the morning and remind you boss that you are still too ill to give your work the attention it requires. Then show up at the office later that morning, find your cubicle and start surfing the net for your *ideal executive assistant!*

It may come as a surprise to your boss that you are at work and yet not working. This, however, should not be of concern. That you showed up is remarkable due to the condition your scurvy has reduced you to. Most of the time, when employees call in sick, they never appear anywhere near their workplace. You, on the other hand, have come to work *even though you can't work!* This will secretly delight your boss and win you definite points! If your boss, at times, still seems skeptical about your illness, groan with pain on occasion. Ask her for a hot cup of herbal tea, a heating pad and a tall glass of orange juice. Wearing pajamas also might help to augment your plight. If your coworkers seem worried about contracting your mysterious illness, allay their fears by assuring them that your affliction, according to your doctor, isn't contagious and that it typically only affects the crews of Renaissance sailing vessels!

Establishing your cubicle as your private space is paramount to getting through the next phase of *Faking Smart!* You are creating a bubble—a private bubble from which to operate. When you bring on an assistant, the bubble is complete!

What is Loyalty?

"Giving someone a job is to give someone something to do."
K.W.A. 1952

There are several ways for you to find and employ a loyal assistant. Under the current business climate (as you well know) it is difficult to find a job; therefore, thanks to our economy's present gloomy forecast, the labor pool is ripe for you to exploit and extract an eager, hard-working helper. Your first thought may be to get right on the web and search out a plum, professional executive assistant. This, however, is the last thing you should do! Professional executive assistants typically come with lofty demands like health insurance and vacation time, stable and safe work environments, 401k plans and consistent pay. *In other words... a professional is the LAST person you want to bring on board!* We suggest finding alternative ways of employing an effective assistant. Here are a number of tested and proven methods:

Foreign exchange students. Many high schools offer foreign exchange programs to introduce students from "foreign shores" to a comprehensive and wide-ranging American cultural experience. These students have flexible schedules and are encouraged by both their host families and teachers to get out and experience new things during their stay in our country. Like ripe, low-hanging fruit, these students are easy pickings if you present yourself in a professional and amicable fashion. Go ahead and contact any nearby high school and introduce yourself as a corporate liaison intent on offering one of these eager, young visitors a "fully-accredited" (affidavits of international accreditation are available through the *Faking Smart!* website, although, temporarily, we are out of this specific form) six-week internship in the exciting and vibrant field of executive assistantship! Make it clear that, while not necessarily monetarily rewarding (this is a non-paying internship), the student is certain to receive the experience of a lifetime while taking a short, but fun, diversion into the "real-time" world of corporate America. With the completion of some superficial paperwork you'll have yourself a devoted and loyal companion, one ready to give everything for this exclusive adventure in the trenches of American big business. *Plus, you get a helper with a cool accent!*

The elderly or retired sector. With the advancements of science and the eradication of many debilitating diseases, people are living longer and more productive lives than ever before. The result is the development of a large labor supply of the retired and elderly who are open and willing to go back to work, whether to contribute to their meager social security payments or to relieve their desperate lack of activity and socialization. This resource offers you a possibility for giving a retiree a sense of purpose while in return gaining loyalty and trust and the knowledge and wisdom that old people are said to have acquired.

Whatchu lookin' at? Abi & me have seen your kind come & go over the centuries.

Single mothers and the recently divorced. Due to a rise in divorce rates, a substantial sector of our nation's labor pool is filled with women who find themselves suddenly struggling to understand the job market. They have little or no job experience, immediate need for income, and grim prospects for employment above low-paying service sector jobs or the fast-food treadmill. There are many ads on the Internet from single mothers looking for a chance to prove themselves in the workplace, and answering one of these ads might land you an honorable work companion that fits all your requirements. As for women who are recently divorced, often times you will stumble across a notice on the web for group therapy sessions concerned with managing the stress and economics of spousal separation. If you are a woman, paying a visit to one of these sessions is a great way to test your luck! Enter one of these meetings as a "seasoned" divorcee who has been through the wringer and has made it to the other side, happy and empowered. You are attending the meeting, you should relate, *"to give a job and to give hope to someone who has found herself in the same place I once did."* It is a good bet that you will quickly find a trusting and loyal partner from this pool, for kindred spirit is the key to binding devotion and sacrifice—*and low starting pay!*

Work-release programs and ex-cons. As many current and former prisoners know, *it's tough finding a job*. Not only are prisoners and ex-cons underemployed due to the stigma associated with having been convicted of criminal activity, they are often denied entry into a conventional workplace due to a lack of modern cubical-based skills and training. Scouring the state and city criminal system, consequently, is a great way of bringing an underappreciated and motivated (*and* potentially imposing) assistant into your fold. Looking into the prison system's list of released convicts may also produce unexpected rewards. Due to an increase in the prosecution of white-collar criminals, several skilled former office workers have passed through the prison system, many of whom were top CEOs in some of the biggest companies in the United States. A great many of these white-collar criminals find stable and rewarding work hard to come by, so any means by which they can get back into a corporate environment proves extremely alluring. Of these candidates you might strike it rich by scoring a former CEO as your assistant; one with a dandy Rolodex that might, someday, help you out in a pinch!

Laid-off financial sector. Since the bursting of the financial bubble, scores of investment savvy personnel are in a desperate search for stable employment. You might, through the course of your life, have made the acquaintance of one or more of these bright yet naive individuals, and by making a call or two or by sending out a couple of emails you might reel in a person of exceptional intelligence, high loyalty and talent. The trick for employing someone laid-off from the financial sector is to offer a low base pay with the promise of a potential for an incredibly high year-end bonus. By establishing this tentative, shared understanding, you have the opportunity to win an assistant that is prepared to work long hours, tackle difficult deadlines and comply with outrageous demands while settling for a base pay of mere breadcrumbs. (Be sure to supplement this person's wages with some sort of legalized depressant or stimulant, like cigarettes or alcohol… or any combination of the two.)

Actors/artists. The last sector you might explore to produce a worthy assistant is the creative arts scene. While exploring this pool of candidates for an assistant carries with it a certain level of risk, the results may prove pleasantly surprising. The old expression *"Don't quit your day job…"* is a reality many artists and actors struggle with. While they may wish to be working on enduring creative efforts that will survive critical scrutiny for centuries to come, their pocket books routinely come up thin when reality comes knocking on the door for rent at the end of the month. In other words, artists don't want to be doing anything that may interfere with their craft, but to survive *they must!* And this is where you come in. If you can rein in one of these social renegades to lend you a hand as an assistant at InCredidata (or wherever it is you work) you would be bringing in someone with an attitude of self-righteousness, discontent and a prickly resentment toward anything that doesn't serve to further his or her artistic goals. What better attitude could you wish for in an assistant? If you can tolerate a daily inundation of snarky indifference, glutinous self-pity and dead-pan cynicism, you just may have hit upon the perfect assistant and a grand companion to help you through the six-week program! Plus, you're directly contributing to the arts scene in your community by employing an artist! *(And, as things go, this may work to your advantage when tallying up tax deductions at the end of the year.)*

Finding a good assistant is key to reaching a turning point in the *Faking Smart! Six-Week Program*. Once you hire and install this new employee your life is made immeasurably easier by the buffer zone, or *wall of impregnability*, you establish between you and the rest of the office. You'll notice that your work load is much more manageable, the information that reaches you is the information *you* want, and you will quickly learn how to enjoy the barrier you've set between you and your boss and co-workers. By delegating work to your assistant you avoid having to immerse yourself in the dull activities that are an inseparable part of nearly every entry-level corporate job. A good assistant allows you to stretch out and feel more at home… *while you're at work!*

Again, if you retain an exchange student as your assistant, you will not need to worry about providing pay. This student, you should make clear, will be rewarded through *Faking Smart!* internship credits that will be processed and transferred through our main offices after a period of many months and, perhaps, years. For an assistant that demands weekly payment, be sure to pay well and pay on time (within a day or two after receiving reported hours). If you are short on funds and find this difficult to fulfill, here's a clever way to raise a quick buck: go to Craigslist and place an ad stating that you have an employee (your assistant) with an incurable case of Heisenberg's Syndrome, and that you need cash, lots of cash, *fast,* to pay for a rare and expensive medical treatment not covered by your employee health insurance policy. Use the money from donations to pay off your assistant, then, after you've finished with the six-week program return this money with the salary increase you receive once you become a VP! *It's that simple!* When you return the money, state that you now know, with certainty, that your employee does not have Heisenberg's Syndrome. Mention that a diagnosis of Heisenberg's Syndrome is rare and usually a false positive, and this is where you and the physicians failed in their diagnosis. When the diagnosis came in "negative," it was assumed that the opposite was true. Hence the mistake… When the donors receive this "apology" they will have no option but to scratch their heads, re-deposit their money and forget the whole thing happened!

Day Four: Install Your Assistant

Take an hour or so this Thursday morning to acquaint your employee with his or her new surroundings. Follow the model of your own orientation at the company and make sure your assistant is answerable only to you. Whatever you do, do not introduce your assistant to your boss. The reason for this is to keep their relationship detached and undefined. If your boss acts concerned, tell her that this is only a temporary situation to handle your work backlog. Mention that your assistant is ICWU (International Cubicle Workers Union) approved and offer an affidavit to this effect. (The by-laws, manifesto and assistant's affidavit of the ICWU are available for order at www.fakingsmart.com. Currently, our only copies are in Hungarian and we have very few of these left.) Be reminded that your boss has offered you the breathing room to pick out and pimp your cubicle… consequently, hiring your own assistant won't be a hard pill for her to swallow. Remember, you are *Faking Smart!* You are the hotshot on the floor. Now live up to your reputation and make your assistant feel at home. Get him or her a small desk and place it right next to yours. Provide your new assistant with a laptop and then let your assistant loose on the stack of papers and operations binders that you didn't take the time to read when first hired. Have your assistant review the material and type a report that will accompany a small presentation to be given for you at the end of the day!

Remember, *a busy employee is a loyal employee*, so give your assistant as much work as you can. Offices are never at a loss for providing busy work *(like reports and forms)* for their employees, so don't be lenient when it comes to finding constructive tasks to be completed. Any time you give this assistant work you are cutting down on the time *you* need to spend doing it, so don't be concerned when you see your assistant up to the neck in papers while you've got nothing better to do than check up on sports scores and review your Internet dating site for potential hook-ups. If you establish a firm understanding that you are the boss, you are better off in the long run.

Whatever you do, *do not* reveal to your new assistant the fact that you are participating in one of the world's leading career-building programs. The virtue of the *Faking Smart! Six-Week Program* is best appreciated when others are unaware that you are associated with this firmament-cracking method of career advancement, and keeping this knowledge from your closest co-worker is paramount for the success of this program.

So, you have your new assistant, you've pimped your cubicle and everyone is looking up to you with envy because of the assertive way in which you handle yourself. It may seem like you have a moment to relax, but this is far from the truth. On Friday, day five, lay the foundations for laying-off your boss!

Friday: *Surprise!*

Everyone loves a party, and today you're the center of attention while the entire floor helps you to celebrate your birthday! Remember, even if it isn't your real birthday today, be a good sport and pretend that it is. Also, be sure to keep the planning of your party a secret from everyone except your assistant. Here is a list of things you will need for this fifth day of work:

1. Four-dozen gourmet doughnuts (depending on the number of co-workers in your office floor... two doughnuts per employee.)
2. 5 extra-large delivery pizzas with assorted toppings.
3. Twenty helium balloons with your name on them reading: "HAPPY BIRTHDAY _____!" (insert your name here)
4. A large birthday cake. Have this message written in frosting: WHY CAN'T YOU BE OUR BOSS? ALL OUR LOVE AND BEST WISHES, THE FLOOR STAFF!

Give this list to your assistant Thursday night, and instruct him or her where to acquire each of the above items. The following morning start things off by having your assistant distribute the doughnuts to the floor staff. Just before lunch break have the pizzas delivered, then, just as lunch seems to be wrapping up, have your assistant bring out the cake with a couple of deadwoods and a brainiac or two (deadwoods and brainiacs will be described later in the six-week program) to help with the "Happy Birthday" song. Act surprised! If you can, for dramatic effect, attempt to shed a tear and then make a brief speech thanking everyone for putting this surprise party together.

There's no better way to increase office moral than to throw a party, and today you are doing just that. After the cake's been cut and your manager comes out to settle things down, relax and enjoy the attention you've attracted. Ask your manager if she was the one that planned this excellent party. No? Either way, show how this makes you proud to be on the InCredidata (or whatever company it is) team and that this whole experience makes you want to work harder and be more productive. Now, assign whatever work you need done for the day to your assistant and then leave the office early to beat traffic home. You're going to want to kick up your heels this evening and feel the warm gooey feeling you get when you've successfully finished Week One of the *Faking Smart! Six-Week Program*.

During the next couple of days, be sure to schedule a relaxing game of Polo or organize a quiet foxhunt with some friends while preparing for Week Two. Also, you might want to pick up a pair of sturdy climbing boots for the coming week, because you don't want to slip when taking your first steps on your new corporate ladder!

You've survived Week One. Good work! Now, get ready to dive into the next phase of the *Faking Smart! Six-Week Program*. And remember, we're with you every step of the way… as you plod through mud, mist, mosquitoes, pits of venomous snakes and the ponds of poisonous toads we're right behind you, pointing your way through that unforgiving corporate jungle so, in the end, you emerge beaten, bruised, gnawed on, and drained… but alive! That's right, when you're *Faking Smart!* you *are* the survivor! You've got that confidence and glow. When you're *Faking Smart!* you're never voted off the island… you're king or queen of that new strip of sand we like to call Vice President Beach!

Week 2
WHO MOVED MY CORPORATE LADDER?

"I've never met a corporate ladder I didn't want to climb."
K.W.A., from his autobiography,
A History of Genius

WAY TO GO! IT'S YOUR SECOND WEEK on the job and not only have you established a dominant presence among your co-workers, but you've made it through enough of the *Faking Smart! Six-Week Program* to be able to say *"Hey, Faking Smart! isn't as hard as I thought it would be!"*

Your Week at a Glance

So, you have pimped your cubicle, installed an assistant and settled in with your job on the floor. It may appear that the world is your oyster and that this may be the perfect time to kick back, relax and reap the rewards of having established yourself at your entry-level position… *but this is the last thing you should be thinking about!* No, just because you are comfortable and content doesn't mean that it's time to rest. Your second week on the job is one of the most pivotal in the *Faking Smart! Six-Week Program* and we are here to hold your hand as you make your way through one of the most crucial and important sections that will get you a vice presidency *only five weeks from today!*

There are three main goals you need to accomplish in this phase of the six-week program. First, you will need to gain a working knowledge of what a corporate ladder is and its role in modern business. Second, you will need to develop an understanding of the dynamics of a typical, corporate workplace floor (such as your own). Lastly, you must adhere to the rigid timetable of tasks and tactics that we have laid out for you so that by Friday you will have installed yourself as the new office manager, complete with brass nameplate and notice of increase in pay.

By getting through this phase of the *Faking Smart! Six-Week Program*, you will have proved to yourself that you are able to let us guide you through to your ultimate goal: *becoming a VP!* Now follow our instructions and in no time you'll be spinning in your boss's chair with a grin on your face as you repeat boldly: *"Faking Smart!, where would I be without you!?"*

The Corporate Ladder, Demystified

You've heard everybody talk about it. You've heard jokes told about it and perhaps even heard a tale or two about others who have climbed it, but did you ever pause to think about what a corporate ladder actually is, and more importantly, how you could get a foot firmly planted on the first rung? Almost everywhere you turn in our culture there are references to corporate ladders: how exciting they are to climb and how great the view is when one reaches the top. What you don't often hear, however, is the darker side to this corporate mainstay: how difficult it is to place your first step, and once you're there... *how easy it is to fall off.* The fact that ladders have become lighter, cheaper and sturdier hasn't made any difference in the hardship people are continuing to find in implementing them at their places of work, and shameful office superstitions continue to flourish, like the *"old corporate wives' tale"* about how bad luck will strike when someone walks underneath one, or how unfolding a corporate ladder in an office is as disruptive to cosmic energy, or karma, as is opening an umbrella indoors. But if we cast folklore into its legitimate domain, i.e., into that of gossip and myth, and look at corporate ladders with a rational eye, we quickly learn that, through proper institutional practice, corporate ladders hold a basic and utilitarian place in the lives of everyone trying to navigate their way through the demanding levels of American business hierarchy.

"So what, exactly, is a corporate ladder?"

To get a brief overview of what a corporate ladder is, one need only look up the key word "ladder" on the Internet, or search on a big box store website and you will discover just about everything you ever thought you would need to know and more about this mystical topic: the difference between expansion ladders and folding ladders, step ladders (*footstools*) vs. painter's ladders, foreign vs. domestic brands… rope ladders vs. Ladder Day Saints.

To speak frankly, most executives of major U.S. companies have individual corporate ladders purchased long before starting their steady and sometimes precarious climbs toward prominence at their firms. Once, after a protracted and demanding slog, an executive has ascended to his or her rung of entitlement, the ladder is usually folded up and stored in a nearby closet where it remains until the executive gets a promotion, is "let go" from personnel or chooses to retire voluntarily. The ladder, however, may make a rare appearance if a question arises among competing ranks over the executive's claim of legitimacy. During such a crisis the ladder is removed from the closet, dusted off and set upright in answer to the challenge. An authoritative nod in the direction of the "executive's rung" is usually enough to quash even the most vociferous of dissenters—such is the power the corporate ladder wields.

It is a very special moment when an executive ascends to the highest rung and such an achievement signifies the coronation of a new president or CEO! A huge party is thrown, consequently, in his or her honor, and the occasion offers all the opportunity to participate in insider trading (trading baseball cards and comic books and stuff like that instead of working, like they should be.) The celebration will inevitably carry on for days, weeks and in some cases years, and will contribute to extended campaigns of corporate card sharking, business brigandage and presidential privateering. Thereafter the CEO or president will be called to task, reined in and forced out. Company assets are then sold off, layoffs instigated and a return to ledger-book scrutiny prefigures a new ascendant to the CEO/presidential throne.

When a CEO or president finally leaves a company, another party is given where he or she is awarded a golden parachute to help him or her fall back to the ground from the previously high position on the ladder. A golden parachute isn't really a parachute, however, (a real parachute probably wouldn't open in time) it is a golden replica of a parachute which they can exchange at a pawnshop or jeweler's showroom for a billion dollars. After the CEO or president leaves his or her job, the person on the next rung now has a place to reach... where he or she will take the place of the out-going CEO. But remember, anybody with a corporate ladder can claim that job. It's just a matter of getting out one's ladder and seeing who gets to the top first!

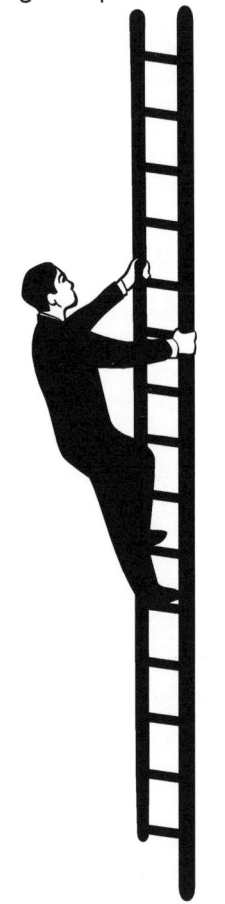

It is wise for those considering climbing a corporate ladder to pick one up! The fact that you have a ladder is motivation to climb it, and when participating in the *Faking Smart! Six-Week Program*, procuring your own ladder is indispensable when it comes to reaching your goal of attaining the VP rung! With the advent of an expanding global economy, companies that have implemented broad layoff plans have provided a boon for individuals seeking cheap and reliable corporate ladders... if you don't mind getting a used one, that is, or one that is somewhat dirty or (unfortunately) bloody.

Once you obtain your corporate ladder, it becomes simply a matter of deciding how quickly you wish to ascend, and by participating in the *Faking Smart! Six-Week Program* the answer is... straight to the middle—*the VP rung*—in six week's time! Yes, the corporate ladder offers you the perfect opportunity and means in which to make it to VP status at your company in six weeks. Let us keep our eye on that goal while you climb your ladder using a job-advancement method proved to be one of the best there is... the *Faking Smart!* method!

The Modern Corporate Worker Floor

By opening your eyes to the mysterious world of the corporate worker floor you will not only *feel smarter* but you will *look smarter* as you become familiarized with the important dynamics of your work environment (the way your office really functions) and utilize these group fundamentals to facilitate the targeting and obtaining of our goals. Up till now you've been asked to fake smart in less obtrusive ways, by depending, largely, on your own merits. This week the tedious and comprehensive work of the FSRI comes into its most shocking and awesome effect... the result, a real-time promotion and your first step up the corporate ladder toward the coveted title of... you know it, VP!

Dynamics of Your Workplace

It may not seem this way at first, but your workplace is actually built on a well-ordered system of individuals and groups with defined stations of importance, all interacting to make your company run and appear busy. That person you saw today delivering mail around to different offices and departments... if he weren't there, how would VPs and presidents get the mail they were waiting for? Who would deliver the important contracts that needed signing? Knowing what people do in your office and what their responsibilities are is critical to gaining a vague understanding of where *you* fit in and what you and your coworkers actually need to appear to be doing on the floor to make your company function. You don't have to know exactly what the dynamic of your office is, but to know, simply, that a dynamic exists. Gaining this realization puts you head and shoulders above your competition (your coworkers) and places you in optimal position for a *Faking Smart!*-style promotion.

The Workplace Pyramid

To begin your lesson on the dynamics of your workplace, it is best to start off by describing the cultural make-up of people around you. The following pyramid describes the five levels of hierarchy that comprise your immediate entry-level environment: the manager, of course, at the top, and the deadwood and new hires making up the base. If you are ever in a situation where you need to remember where you stand in relation to your coworkers, just review this **workplace pyramid** for quick and accurate reference.

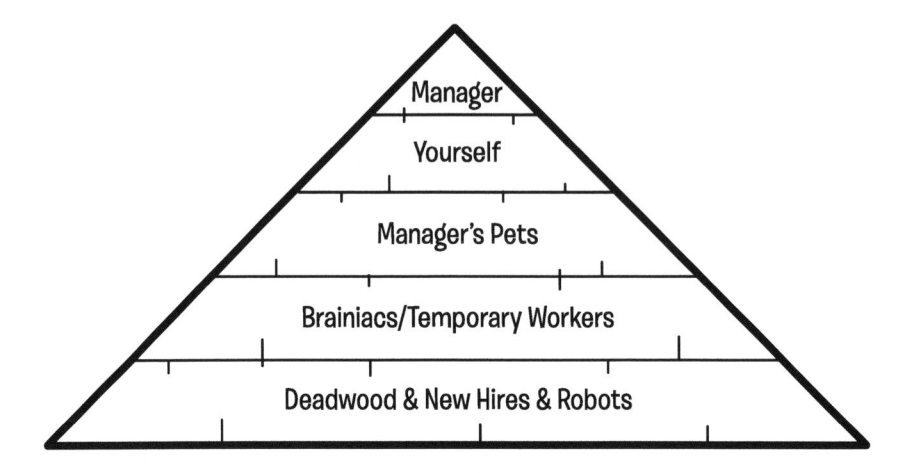

```
                    Manager
                    Yourself
                 Manager's Pets
            Brainiacs/Temporary Workers
         Deadwood & New Hires & Robots
```

The manager. The manager is the person with the highest level of authority on the floor of most corporate customer service, data-entry or order desk departments. The manager (or managers, in some cases) has the responsibility of hiring and firing floor personnel, motivating and encouraging corporate work ethic, listening to and getting feedback from employees on projects and, finally, reporting productivity and outcome to the higher ups (the "higher ups" being those whom the manager reports to [unseen in this workplace pyramid]). The manager also has the responsibility to make irrational hiring decisions, appear perpetually hung-over, play favoritism and discourage creative thinking.

Yourself. You, as a clear office presence and maverick operator, stand just below the manager in the workplace hierarchy. Although deemed a beneficent outlaw in the eyes of co-workers and janitorial staff, you are next in line to move into management responsibility, and it's not due to experience, networking or excellent job skills… it's due to the fact that you're *Faking Smart!*, and consequently you have an appreciable advantage in fulfilling the role of inheritor to your boss's position. If it weren't for your participation in the *Faking Smart! Six-Week Program*, you would be stuck down at the bottom of the pyramid with the deadwoods and new hires. But by *Faking Smart!* you maintain the *edge* by being backed by countless hours of research at our institute and by carrying the shared wisdom of a maverick and captain of industry—Karl Wolfbooks Ager—who has revolutionized the way we look at modern business.

[If you have friends, be sure to tell them about our astounding six-week program. Remember, if you refer someone to our program, and they buy our books and products and mention your name as a reference, you automatically become a member of the Faking Smart! Six-Week Program *Referral Club and receive a free congratulatory email expressing our thanks and best wishes in your career!]*

The manager's pets. Manager's pets occupy the third tier of the workplace pyramid because, although behind you in line for the job, they threaten your likelihood of becoming the next manager by simply believing themselves to be "tight" with the boss, and consequently next on the list. Like teacher's pets, manager's pets are just as whiney, obnoxious and blindly ambitious. Their deep-rooted feelings of entitlement cause them to consistently thwart the goals sought by many an honest and well-intentioned *Faking Smart!* participant. While much of the communication between pet and manager is kept hidden, a few telltale signs can unmask such an employee. Anyone seen spending a particularly long time sitting near the manager—whispering to and laughing at inside jokes—is most likely a pet, especially if, when approached, he or she clams up and slinks away in typical pet fashion. Many pets find privilege in lunching with the boss, too, while others can be found partying with the head of the floor out at the bars after work. A particularly bad situation arises when a manager or boss is dating someone from the center floor. These pets should be considered **Super Pets** by nature of their elite insider status. Favoritism is lavished upon such employees, so super pets may pose the biggest obstacle when attempting to take your boss's job. Research at the FSRI has discovered that keeping a close eye on manager's pets is essential to fulfilling this phase of the six-week program. The *Faking Smart! Six-Week Program*, however, is skillfully designed to circumvent this ruthless tier of the workplace pyramid, and if followed correctly, the tactics and techniques in this chapter allow for these current pets to become *your* pets when you take over the reins of power at the end of the week.

Brainiacs and temporary workers. These are your friends. This group forms a large portion of any entry-level corporate service floor. They seem to work at their current position merely to occupy time while waiting for bigger and better things in their lives. Brainiacs and temp workers, for some reason, are quick to judge the antics of *Faking Smart!* practitioners as amusing, if not entertaining. These employees are indifferent to workplace turbulence and observe the chaos your presence creates with affection and as possible material for future novels, screenplays and performance art.

Deadwood, new hires and robots. This tier of the workplace hierarchy is the most benign and unthreatening to the practitioner of the *Faking Smart! Six-Week Program*. As for new hires, their daily work is mostly concerned with the stress involved in doing a good job. They are characteristically timid and quick to take orders—i.e., *they are an excellent source of help when you find yourself in need*. Deadwood, for that matter, are also hardworking and affable, but while demonstrating loyalty and company spirit, the deadwood have never found themselves to be a bona fide company "fit" and consequently have relegated themselves to "lifer" status in their current position. Not that they mind much. Deadwood can be characterized as pursuing the delusion that some day they *will* be a company fit, and this is enough motivation to keep them coming to work every day. Lastly, Robots need not be of much concern for the *Faking Smart!* participant. Although robots will take over the world a hundred-and-seven years from now, at present robots' intelligence still lags behind that of humans' and should not be considered as a threat to your next promotion. Do not be afraid of their metallic voices and retractable metal arms either. After some time working with robots you might discover them to be polite and amicable workmates!

Fringe groups. Although unseen in our workplace pyramid, fringe groups should be recognized as having a legitimate presence in any corporate setting. The unique thing about fringe groups is that any one of these loosely formed gangs may have representatives from any and all levels of the pyramid. The smoker fringe group is the best example. In the smoker group you may find a super-pet chatting with a deadwood, a brainiac hanging with a new hire, or, on occasion, you may even catch a manager laughing it up with a robot as they each draw expertly at their cigarettes under the building's fire escape! At some point in the *Faking Smart! Six-Week Program* you may be encouraged to "*pick up a smoke*" and join in this sardonic and witty enclave in attempt to spread a rumor or two. Other fringe groups exist in the pyramid... such as the happy-hour gang, the "company" soccer team, the book club and the poetry slammers. You may be interested in joining one of these other fringe groups, but most them are unimportant and should be avoided at this stage of the *Faking Smart! Six-Week Program*. The last thing you want to do is get back from a company soccer game, rendezvous with your team at the local pub, tip a few back and then find yourself, in a blur of inebriation, telling everyone you're *Faking Smart!*

So, now that you have a general understanding of your workplace dynamic, let us move on to the nuts and bolts of this phase of the *Faking Smart! Six-Week Program*. This part of the program will move quickly, so get ready to jump on the speeding train and let us guide you through Week Two. You can do it. We know you can. When you are *Faking Smart!* you always come out ahead. Trust us, *we know what we're talking about!*

Monday: Establish Your *Faking Smart!* Virtual Presence

So, it's Monday morning and you've arrived at your office bright and early— say around 11a.m. Your cubicle is pimped, your assistant hard at work and you've got a full day ahead of you to get done any and all things that need getting done. *"What needs getting done?"* you might be asking yourself as your eyelids begin to sag and your brain lurches forward toward lunch break and the hours that stand between you and a relaxing night in front of the TV. Creating your *Faking Smart!* blog or Twitter account is what needs to get done today!

That's right, instead of using today to catch up on sleep lost while celebrating the completion of Week One, today your efforts turn full throttle to establish yourself as a professional blogger or Twitterer transmitting your progress in the *Faking Smart! Six-Week Program!*

Why should you be blogging or Twittering... broadcasting your life to all corners of the world, from the smallest of llama herding villages in central Peru to greatest of modern cosmopolitan cities... like Omaha, Winnipeg or Rice Lake, Wisconsin? *You should be blogging or Twittering, simply, because everyone in the world wants to see how you're doing:... what your status update is, how you're getting along with fellow employees, if any of the keys on your computer keyboard consistently jam, if you've got the latest mammalian virus from the person in the opposite cubicle, when your next promotion is scheduled and what you're eating for breakfast on the drive to work?* As you are in one of the most atom-smashing programs known on earth, there is a huge, if not infinite, audience out there that wants to be in constant virtual contact with everything you're doing at every second of the day. Creating your own *Faking Smart!* Twitter account is the perfect means of addressing this certain and inevitable flock of groupies, celebrity-obsessed paparazzi and zealot adherents to everything concerning *Faking Smart!* The same goes for creating a blog!

THINGS TO KEEP IN MIND WHEN PUBLISHING YOUR *FAKING SMART!* UPDATES:

- Be honest when writing about your experiences *Faking Smart!* Your followers will see through it if you're pulling their leg.
- Use pictures and links to videos when creating posts. It's fun reading about someone else's life, but inserting video and pictures into the fold makes for a far more interactive participation between you and your readers.
- Have your assistant set up phony "visitor" accounts so that he or she can comment on your posts in the guise of being a different, and, at times, new contributor. This gives the appearance that people from all over the world are following and commenting on your blog— EXACTLY WHAT YOU WANT!
- Visit other like-minded blogs and Twitter accounts (...perhaps other *Faking Smart!* sites) and participate in their discussion threads. This will ultimately drive traffic back to *your* blog or Twitter posts and earn you (and the FSRI) a wider audience.
- By the end of the day (this Monday), set a goal to obtain 2000 unique URL visits to your blog or Twitter posts. If you can do this, you've completed today's tactic with stellar results!

Remember, when linking on your *Faking Smart!* Twitter updates, be sure you don't link to anything you yourself wouldn't want to see. When Twittering, also make sure to keep your identity a secret; this will help you to avoid any legal tangles that many previous *Faking Smart!* Twitterers have encountered. People want to know you're *Faking Smart!*, just don't tell them where you're doing it and you'll be fine! ***It's that easy!***

Lastly, if you're going to blog, please expend a slight bit of effort to upload some original video! Linking to sites, photos and other blogs is great, but give us the beef! We want to see video! Give the world a view of what it's like commuting to work. Show us a copy of this book as you hold it in front of your monitor—what page are you on? Give us a quick scan of your office, your cubicle and the style in which it's been pimped. Give us a gander at your office's SUPER PET if you can... *legally*. (Have him or her sign a "release of interest" form before your video goes live.) Let your creativity flow, and produce some good content so that everyone else can mark your progress in the six-week program!

Tuesday

The FSRI recommends that you take today to update your blog or Twitter accounts and to just be at work and get a few things done! Yes, you've deserved this break, so soak it all in while you can. Make a few copies at the copier and then ask your boss if you can take "fifteen" to run down to the coffee kiosk and top off your mug. When you return ask your assistant if she or he needs any help, then dive back into whatever it was you were doing earlier.

Take a few calls today (...your assistant will appreciate it). Crunch a few numbers and give a coworker a high five for something cool that happened. Today is your day to get to know what it's like to work on an entry-level corporate floor environment. We want you to smell the smells of working in the good old cubicle grind. Tell your coworker in the next cubicle to "put on his shoes!" Toss a secret message with a paper airplane to a friend of yours at the other end of the floor with a joke about what another coworker is wearing. Basically, today is your day to work as any other cubicle worker would work! Yawn loudly when bored... *enough so that your neighbor has to look around the corner at you with disdain.* Shout at someone on the phone so that your boss is forced to run over and ask what just happened. In other words, learn and live what it means to survive as an entry-level cubicle worker in today's competitive corporate environment... and then call it a day at, say, 4:00 p.m. or so. (Your assistant can mop up any of your unfinished business.) Today you've absorbed what it's like to work as a base employee. *Tomorrow, everything changes.* Tomorrow you begin your rapid march toward the management class, and the things you've learned today will help you to successfully reach your new goals!

Wednesday: Rumor and Hearsay

You'll probably want to come in a little earlier than usual today—say 10-10:30 a.m.—to make sure you pay an important visit to one of the office fringe groups. If you can, during one of the several breaks taken by this group during the day, drop in on the smoker fringe group and politely ask one of its members if it's possible to *"bum a smoke."* When you receive the offered cigarette ask if someone has a light; then light it, draw in the smoke and expel it. (When smoking, be sure not to breathe in the smoke; merely *pretend* to be smoking to fit in with this fringe group. To light your cigarette, place it between your lips and then draw on the filtered end as the flame touches the opposite end. Instead of inhaling, however, draw the smoke into your mouth and then puff it out safely without letting it reach your lungs.) Do this a couple of times to look cool and then let slip a couple of rumors.

Mention, off-handedly, that you are from "corporate" and that you are doing a secret performance audit of your department. The next rumor you need to dispense is the "fact" of an on-going investigation by the FDIC (use whatever acronym you can come up with) into whether or not floor management has participated in fraudulent activity. Lastly, include an off-hand remark about toxic chemicals in the plywood used in the construction of the floor cubicles. Keep these rumors vague yet concise—when you are finished throw your cigarette to the ground and crush it under the heel of your boot.

These tidbits of information, or rumors, will find their way, first, to one of the manager's pets and then on to the manager. Interpretation of this information by the recipients should not be your concern. The FSRI has done extensive and complicated research on the effects of rumors and see them as essential components to the *Faking Smart! Six-Week Program*. Your job is to be the messenger, and we all know that the messenger is never blamed in these instances. Remember to dispense with these rumors effectively and in the way we propose and do not attempt to embellish or add to your list of rumors or you run the risk of "Lying Your Way to VP-ship," which is a completely different and unrelated program, independent of the *Faking Smart! Six-Week Program* and unaffiliated with the FSRI or FSIHL.

Great work! Give yourself a pat on the back for completing the only task required of you today. Now return to your cubicle and update any of your social networking sites and then see what the latest Hollywood gossip is. At the end of this long day, go home and watch an old movie and then get some rest. On second thought, go ahead and uncork a bottle of wine and then take a long bath (if you don't have a bathtub do not attempt to drink wine while taking a shower), then set your alarm for 9:30 a.m. so you can get in some extra sleep and get to the office early—no later than 11:00 a.m.—the next day.

Thursday: *Your big day*

Yes, it is an incontrovertible fact that robots will take over Earth only a little over a century from now. Knowing this will help you to successfully pull off today's tasks. In the InCredidata offices (as in most modern office complexes) there are tens, if not hundreds, of robots zipping around, going up and down elevators, delivering documents and alleviating office drudgery. Robots are commonplace in today's offices, and becoming one for a day will give you the insight into your company that many would go to great lengths to gather.

Before arriving at work, come up with a robot outfit that will prove convincing to both your fellow employees and, most importantly, your boss. Below are three FSRI recommended robot disguises:

The FS3000, or "The Shredder." At the writing of this book, this little fellow was one of the most familiar of the office robots in corporate America. To adopt this disguise all you need is a large square box, a skateboard, some red and green scotch tape, two penlights and some silver paint. Once you've crawled under the silver-painted box, sit squarely on the skateboard and practice scooting around the office, being sure to keep the profile of the box low to the ground so your hands aren't exposed. Remember: the real FS3000 responds to voice commands. The nice thing about this model is that it has no voice actuation... it simply acknowledges commands with an affirmative GREEN light or a negative RED light (your penlights wrapped in green and red scotch tape.) The primary duties of the FS3000 are to shred documents, so cut a paper-length slot in the front panel of the disguise and produce a shredding sound whenever someone inserts any paper. These little buggers are highly utilized throughout the course of the corporate day, so be sure to have plenty of space to store the paper your robot is constantly being fed!

The Corp255, or "The Enforcer." You've probably seen one of these awkward, yet intimidating robots while roaming the company's halls, taking bathroom breaks or when arguing for possession over a cup of yogurt in front of the break room fridge. These robots were designed, primarily, for surveillance, security, delivering termination notices and to assist cafeteria staff (...they are excellent at mashing potatoes and blending smoothies.) Even though the disguise for this robot may prove a little more difficult to pull off, the payoff is high. To successfully disguise yourself as a Corp255 model, you'll need a rectangular box that will cover you from head to waist, a medium-sized goldfish jar, two red-light penlights (your robot's eyes), 12 feet of 8" black, flexible landscaping conduit, silver paint, two prosthetic hooks or retractable grabber claws and a pair of roller skates. The trick to making this disguise work is in knowing how to roller skate, for all of the Corp255 models propel themselves in such a fashion. The other thing to keep in mind is that this model *DOES* simulate human vocalization when communicating, so practice up on your metallic robot voice!

Default robot outfit. If you can't manage to get a hold of a skateboard for the FS3000, or if you don't know how to roller skate to simulate the Corp255 robot's agile movements, then there is always the standby robot prototype trick. For this you'll need about 50' of rolled aluminum foil, some space-age looking sunglasses and a pair of thick-soled boots. Simply encase yourself in this aluminum foil, poke holes for your eyes and nose, put on your sunglasses and, voila, you're a prototype of a new model robot! If anybody asks what kind of robot you are simply state in your metallic robot-like voice that you are such and such a model (make a model number up… it's easy to do!) and that you are on beta trial to see if you're compatible with the InCredidata offices. Bingo! You're now an official robot, free to wander the office halls and assist when requested. Keep in mind that a little bit of acting may be involved when using this outfit. Walk stiffly, if you can, when wrapped in this disguise. Make short, clear statements when addressed (always, with a monotone, metallic voice). You might even put in some time at a telephone desk and field a question or two? Whatever choices you make when appearing as a convincing robot prototype, be sure to be helpful and dispassionate when taking orders from your superiors. If you can manage this, you'll make it through the day with no problem whatsoever!

The Accidental Email

When you arrive at the office Thursday, your big day, make your presence known to your manager by mentioning to her that **you're on jury call** and might be summoned at any time. At your desk, check up on your assistant and make sure he or she has plenty of work, then steal away to the stockroom to dress in your robot disguise. When in you're in the FS3000 outfit, don't be surprised if you're kicked around a bit while you scurry up and down the office aisles and halls. Although invaluable to the functioning of your company, these little shredders are considered a nuisance by many who don't have much paper to shred, i.e. I.T. personnel, other robots and most of the hourly workers on your floor. Take this with a grain of salt, for your mission has broader importance. If you're in a Corp255 disguise, observe the respect (and distance) you're given when rolling up and down the hallways. You'll quickly learn that no one wants to get in the way of *The Enforcer*. If you're in a default, aluminum foil disguise, do your *darnedest* and hope for the best!

Once you've moved around the office floor for a little while and are used to your disguise, pay a visit to your manager's office to see how things are going. Remember, robots are a mainstay in any modern, professional environment, so don't be surprised if your presence among managers and staff goes unnoticed. Believe it or not, this is exactly what you want!

After "shredding" a document or two that your boss has crammed into your paper slot, go into sleep mode by making a high-pitched whirring sound that slowly descends to a low-level drone. *CLICK.* You're asleep! Now, relax and listen. Learn everything you can about your boss. Who does she like or dislike? What does she talk about when on the phone? What kind of impression (or fears) has your boss formed by the rumors you've spread yesterday? Also, try and glean the name of one or two of her confidants—someone your boss is candid with on the phone. Lastly, take a look around and see how your manager has organized her office. Use this information to help you when this office becomes yours! Now wait for her to go to lunch and then *get to work.*

After your boss has closed the office door and locked it, wait a few minutes for the coast to clear, then inch over to the computer monitor and bring up your boss's email application. Press the "NEW" email button and then type in this message addressed to the "friend" you heard your boss talking to: **Gosh, InCredidata (or whatever company it is) is a joke. With the way those idiots are running things upstairs, you wonder if this company will last another six months! See ya later tonight to get drunk (your manager's first name here)**. Now open your manager's address book and cc as many email addresses as you can find—all the company email addresses with as many executives that you can find on file—and then click "SEND." Now, slink back and resume your sleep mode and wait for your boss to return. Once your manager has returned, promptly scoot your way out of the office and go back to the stockroom and change out of your disguise. When you get back to your cubicle sit down, surf the web and update one of your social networking accounts. After several minutes your boss will emerge from her office with a disheveled and panicked expression. *Your boss has most likely been called to her boss's office!* Now, take this time to implement the last tactic of the day.

Toxic Fumes

While your boss is away (presumably immersed in some serious damage control), start commenting on the odd smell you've noticed emanating from the walls of your cubicle. Make your way up and down the aisles while asking this question to most of the staff: *"Can you smell that?—I don't know, I think I feel dizzy or something—man, there's something up with these cubicles!"* At this point cue your assistant to clutch at his or her throat and scream. If you have any green facial make-up, painting your assistant's face may add to the effect. Then shout: *"Holy, sh–! These cubicles are emitting toxic fumes!"*

As this point everyone will be looking to you to make the call. Your manager is away. There's a potential crisis at hand. With a commanding yet steady voice instruct everyone to move towards the exit… *as fast as they possibly can!* "*Get out of here--NOW!*" you might shout above the clamor, "…*while you still have a chance!*" As everyone rushes towards the door, get back to your cubicle and make a couple of calls. First, call your local TV news outlet and inform them of the emergency at hand. Second, call the fire department and hazardous materials squad and let them know that there has been an outbreak of toxic fumes at the InCredidata offices and that many of the employees have shown symptoms of paranoia, lethargy, fatigue and malaise! Now, get outside of the building and stake out the front entrance while you wait for the news crew to arrive. By the time the media team gets to the InCredidata office, things will be busy with fear and excitement. Step up to the news crew when you first get a chance and state clearly that you are not authorized to make any statement, but that you are forced to do so under existing circumstances. Make this statement:

> On behalf of InCredidata (or whatever company it is you happen to be working for) and the dispersed and fleeing floor personnel, with no manager and the potential for a crisis involving the health and wellbeing of our hard-working staff, I had to make the risky but prudent decision to evacuate the office. Even though it may prove, after a brief investigation, that the floor staff was at no time exposed to any harmful chemicals, this decision was made exclusively with the welfare of my fellow employees in mind. Thank you, that is all.

Once the office has been tested and cleared by the Hazmat team, and your assistant has been treated and released with no more than a Percocet and a pat on the back, the day will draw to a close. This is a perfect time to deliver your boss's termination notice and then go up to the executive offices to relate your account of the day's events. By now the media will have gone live, and you'll be regarded as an InCredidata hero for assuming leadership responsibilities and for looking out for the safety of your fellow staff! When delivering your pink slip (you should prepare this pink slip beforehand) to your boss, be sure to call in an Enforcer bot to assist you in punctuating the severity of the moment. Be sure to mention that upper management (*of the FSRI, wink, wink...*) has authorized you to deliver this notice, and that your out-going boss has fifteen minutes to collect her things and leave the building. Remember, your Enforcer is there to keep things under control.

The FSRI recommended template for a professional pink slip is included below:

[Current date]

Dear [your boss's name in full],

It has become the opinion of the human relations office, the executive staff, the President of Operations, the technical support team and our company mascot, that your services are no long required at InCredidata (or whatever company it is.) After a brief but thorough review it has become painfully apparent that due to breaches of conduct we must release you of all responsibilities as Manager of Customer Service (be specific here). This termination of your position at the InCredidata is effective immediately.

This letter of dismissal has not been easy for us to write. Even though we do know how to write, it is never a light task to tell someone that one's hard work and loyalty to a company such as ours has out-served its purpose. We thank you for your time and commitment

to InCredidata and wish you the best in your future endeavors.

Wishing you the best,
From all of us at here at InCredidata.
[Sign and date]

Be sure to print this on pink paper with company letterhead.

Congratulations!

Ultimately, the *Faking Smart! Six-Week Program* is designed so that, in most cases, your boss will read her termination letter and have no recourse but to humbly accept her fate and to leave without incident. (This entire week has driven her to this conclusion.) After she's gone, collect the items from your cubicle in a box and move immediately into your boss's former office and congratulate yourself on a job well done!

It's never simple adjusting to a new work environment, so don't be surprised if you feel a sense of unease or vertigo when settling yourself in the warm seat of a boss that was there only minutes before you. Push these thoughts of self-doubt aside by looking and acting busy! Search through the stack of papers your boss left behind and let out a burst of anger and frustration. Pick up the phone and shout some scathing remark at the imaginary person on the other end of the line and feel the thrill and exhilaration it gives you. Now, ask yourself: *Are you beginning to feel like a manager? Do you look like a manager should look like, and does your image portray someone of discipline and authority? Do you feel like you can make snap decisions and call the shots?*

Relax! These are all things addressed in the next chapter and you shouldn't stress out trying to learn *everything* about your new role today. Before you leave the office you will need to place two calls: the first to facilities management to request that they dismantle your old "pimped out" cubicle (get rid of all the reminders of this stage of the *Faking Smart! Six-Week Program* by donating your old cubicle decorations to the FSRI Cubicles for Children Foundation—address located on our website); the second call you need to make is to company operations to introduce yourself and to tell them that you are the new manager of your floor staff. The transition from floor employee to manager may seem strikingly easy, but this is how companies operate.

As long as operations is confident that "the machine" is still working they have no interest in getting their fingers dirty in the messy process of firing and hiring a replacement for an outgoing manager. *Just the fact that a manager is there and in the office is all they want to know.* While making your brief phone introduction be certain that your pay-scale correction is in the pipeline and that your brass nameplate is on its way.

Friday

When you come into work on Friday, start by organizing your desk and desk drawers and sort through some of the files your old boss left behind. A lot of these files won't be of much importance to you, but keep from throwing this stuff away as it might be of use to the manager who takes the job after you leave in two weeks. Be sure to bring the computer from your old cubicle and have tech-support help set it up. Also, be sure to bring your chair from your old cubicle if it is nicer than the one your boss was using. Remember the importance of a good office chair: *"If you aren't healthy, comfortable and relaxed at work, why work at all?"*

Once everyone has arrived, get the floor together for an "introduction to their new manager pep talk!" Introduce yourself and your assistant and then tell everyone that you appreciate their hard work and that as a team you hope that everyone can work together to make the service floor the best it can be by continuing to present themselves with professionalism and "good old InCredidata pride." Get everyone juiced up with some spontaneous InCredidata cheer (*"We're number one,"* blah, blah, blah) and then send them back to their cubicles for a good, long day of work.

Wasn't that easy? As a manager, one of your responsibilities is to function as cheerleader to your employees, and if you do this well, work gets done. Although many business schools claim that cheerleading is all a manager does, the FSRI has determined that there are many more subtleties to the job, which we address in Week Three. Being a manager may be tricky at times, but when you're a participant in the *Faking Smart! Six-Week Program* you get a quick lesson on one of the best management methods out there—*The Faking Smart! 12 Point Plan for Effective Business*

Management—which has transformed management in ways nobody could ever imagine!

As for the rest of the day, take it easy. Float in and out of the office with a cup of coffee in your hand and smile and nod when people ask you questions. Lean up against a cubicle and look concerned when an employee tells you how slow his computer is working. Give a cute employee a wink. And don't forget to "drift" up to the executive offices and show your face around town. You're part of the elite club now, so don't be bashful. If you're lucky you'll be dragged into a re-training seminar to get the new spin on your place in the company. You'll be given a thick binder of policy information and a stack of papers to sign (...perfect work for your assistant). If you can squeeze in a massage during lunch, do it, then take some time to think about the "look" you'll need for next Monday's start at a full week of real management work.

When your brass nameplate gets sent down, your day is complete. Instruct your assistant to close up shop at the specified hour and head for home. You've done everything that could be expected of you, so go out and celebrate. Give that cute employee a call if you like and see if he or she cares to join you for a drink. *(You have all the phone numbers on your database!)*

You've made it to manager. You are at the top of your game. Now prepare for next week's crash course in business management where you will begin to understand what it really takes to learn a management style that sets itself apart from all others. By participating in the *Faking Smart! Six-Week Program,* you have nothing to fear. You are in the hands of experts who have researched and perfected a system of corporate ladder climbing that, until recently, no one has dared consider feasible. When *Faking Smart!*, the power of promotion is in your hands. By letting us sculpt you to pursue the goals we deem important, you are taking part in a fail-safe program to become the fastest and most complete VP possible. Good work! You know you can do it, you just don't know that you knew!

> [FACT: Stanizlaw Koznzk, a Polish industrialist and brothel investor, was the first person to implement a corporate ladder in his day-to-day business. In 1856, during a rash of worker unrest, Stanizlaw came up with a blue-print for an executive escape route system that would allow the CEO

and upper management to "slip out the back" in the event of any uprising. Where one stood on the "corporate ladder" was a metaphor for how high one stood in the company, and consequently, how likely that person would be to survive such a revolt. When no uprising took place, Koznzk discovered that the space where the escape ladder stood would provide an ideal parking area for his carriage. Thus was born the first documented implementation of the "Executive Parking" sign, an aspect of early corporate life that remains to this day.]

Week 3
HAIL TO THE CHIEF!

SO YOU'VE MADE THE QUICK TRANSITION to your new management position. Great work! When you're *Faking Smart!* the power to control your corporate destiny is limited only by the degree in which you choose to follow our program. Week by week you draw closer to our goal, to make you a VP and to acquire the *power of unlimited horizontal job potential*. By becoming manager you have succeeded in climbing the next rung of your personal corporate ladder of success. With each additional step your vision of the company becomes clearer and your ease at *Faking Smart!* becomes more and more effortless. When you are *Faking Smart!* you are one step ahead of the pack!

The FSRI (*Faking Smart!* Research Institute):
"Taking over your future so you don't have to worry about it!" ™

Way back in 2009, before I, Karl Wolfbrooks Ager, the author of this book, conceived of an institute that would design and promote the revolutionary ideas of *Faking Smart!*, I had only one thing in mind: *to build a building large enough for hundreds, if not thousands of employees and visitors... then figure out what to do with it after it was finished.* As the last piece of drywall went up and the last window was installed, I worked furiously to individually test all electrical outlets for live current, to make sure that each and every toilet flushed properly and that every break room was stocked with a small, smelly refrigerator containing a paper bag of gooey and indeterminable contents. I also made sure that one wall in each and every room was decorated with the same pastel replica of a Monet painting. Then, after installing "FSRI" in cool, big letters on the front of the building and deciding that the theories of *Faking Smart!* would be taught here, I knew that it would only be a matter of time before people would be drawn to the institute and to the incredible, ground-breaking research it was soon to conduct.

I was right!

Within six months the number of employees at the FSRI had more than doubled. One year later the number of employees was anywhere from four to 1500! Out of sheer genius and determination my vision was finally becoming reality! The reputation of our institute was gaining global visibility at a pace no other institute of its kind had seen before. Quietly, and without much fanfare, the FSRI, to my great delight, made the 2009 *Fortune Finders Top 100* list where it has remained in the exclusive *Elite Top Fifty Club* ever since.

By 2010, with such unheard of rapid growth and success, new and serious measures were taken to insure the expanding legacy of the FSRI. During the spring of that year, upon one of my illuminating epiphanies, the first courses were offered by a new branch of the institute called the *Faking Smart!* Institute for Higher Learning. Today the FSIHL boasts fully accredited four-week Bachelor's and three-week Master's of Science degree programs in *Faking Smart!*, attracting students and researchers from all walks of life, including business leaders, professional athletes, talk-show hosts and heads-of-state.

Not only does the FSIHL manage the hundreds and thousands of students that shuffle quickly in and out of its doors, but the FSIHL also functions as in-house publisher for the astonishing array of pamphlets and brochures that the FSRI kicks out. Utilizing the synergy of these two institutes, I maximized the efficiency with which *Faking Smart!* was disseminated around the globe. The result is the FSRI you see today, with somewhere near 2,000 employees, or so, with offices in all known nations—in Europe, China, Brazil, Cairo, Iceland, Eastern Germany and Norway!

With growth has come prestige, and with prestige has come the great comfort you have in knowing that *you* are participating in a program based on the rudimentary theories that are changing the landscape of the way business is done today! By reading this book and taking part in the *Faking Smart! Six-Week Program*, you are at the cutting edge of career potential. Ask any one of the over two zillion people who have purchased our products or participated in our programs. Who knows, maybe the person sitting across from you in the bus can vouch for *Faking Smart!*? Is he wearing glasses? Is she carrying a corporate ladder? Trust your instincts... it all leads back to *Faking Smart!*

A Management Scheme Based on Rock-Hard Science

A week or two after the construction on the FSRI building was complete, it came to my attention that there was something missing in the solid, yet fledgling, theory of *Faking Smart!* Hours and hours of examination and review of earlier writings revealed a hole in my thought process: *I hadn't come up with a demonstrable and proven method of business management to apply toward a real-world business environment.* The realization of this lapse was devastating, and I quickly came up with a way to address this flaw in my research.

What followed was a long weekend spent working and re-working my theories on the backs of credit card receipts and on the cardboard covers of empty pizza boxes. Using video games and old Radiohead CDs to spark the creative process I stumbled, early one Saturday morning, upon a stunning and conclusive revelation. Using the gifts of science to validate this discovery, I devised a schematic that would put to rest any doubt that my theories were unsound. The result was the **Karl Wolfbrooks Ager Schematic for Faking Smart!** *in Business Management:*

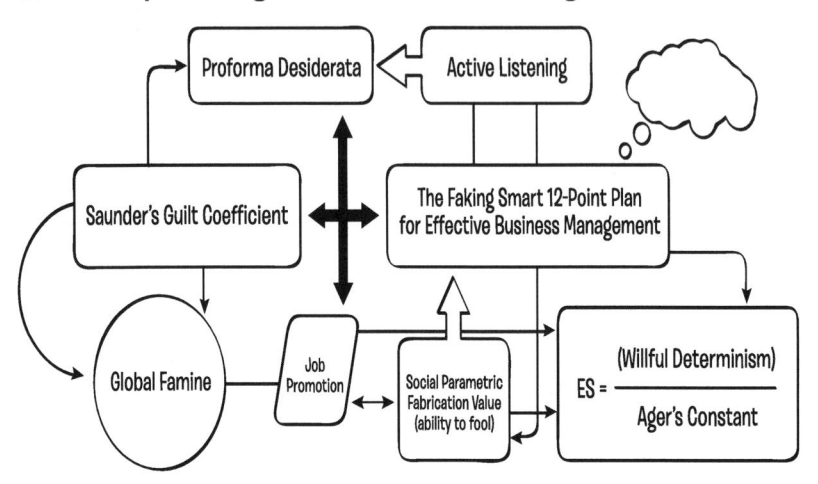

```
    ┌──────────────────┐     ┌──────────────────┐
    │Proforma Desiderata│ ◄── │ Active Listening │
    └──────────────────┘     └──────────────────┘
             ▲                        │
             │                        ▼
    ┌──────────────────┐  ┌───────────────────────────┐
    │Saunder's Guilt   │ ◄►│The Faking Smart 12-Point  │
    │Coefficient       │   │Plan for Effective         │
    │                  │   │Business Management        │
    └──────────────────┘   └───────────────────────────┘
             │                        ▲
             ▼                        │
    ┌──────────┐  ┌────┐  ┌──────────────┐  ┌──────────────────┐
    │  Global  │──│Job │──│Social        │  │  (Willful        │
    │  Famine  │  │Pro-│◄►│Parametric    │  │   Determinism)   │
    │          │  │mo- │  │Fabrication   │  │ES = ─────────────│
    │          │  │tion│  │Value         │  │  Ager's Constant │
    │          │  │    │  │(ability to   │  │                  │
    │          │  │    │  │ fool)        │  │                  │
    └──────────┘  └────┘  └──────────────┘  └──────────────────┘
```

After submitting this schematic to the editor of my peer-reviewed *Faking Smart!* journal, I hoped that things would begin to move quickly. *I was right!* When the schematic, to my surprise, was published in the following month's edition, a new universe opened up for the prospects of *Faking Smart!* This led the way for one of the most important developments in the entire *Faking Smart!* system: the *Faking Smart! 12 Point Plan for Effective Business Management.* The rest is history!

This chapter is devoted to giving you, the reader and participant in the *Faking Smart! Six-Week Program*, the benefit of a clear and concise description of a management plan that would change the face of business and industry for the foreseeable future. Taken with a moderate degree of seriousness, this plan is guaranteed to make you stand out as manager at your firm. In today's competitive and developing corporate environment it is essential that you stand out—make yourself noticed—and *Faking Smart!* makes certain that you to do just that!

Manage Like a Pro

"The trick to unlocking your management potential is, first, to find a key... then see if it fits."

—Karl Wolfbrooks Ager,
from his address to the July, 2010 undergraduate class,
FSIHL Commencement Ceremony

So, you have moved yourself into your new office or expanded cubicle area, the facilities people have installed your brass nameplate, you've set up your corporate ladder in plain sight and you've relocated your assistant to an area where you have immediate yet buffered communication with him or her. Everything is in place. The only thing you require now is a quick lesson on managing the employees on the floor who are in constant need of your attention and advice.

In Week Three of the *Faking Smart! Six-Week Program* you should concentrate on achieving two basic goals: first, you should prepare yourself to obtain rudimentary understanding of the *Faking Smart! 12 Point Plan For Effective Business Management* (this will allow you the opportunity to arbitrarily apply some of the plan's 12 points in real-time situations); secondly, you will be asked to circulate and network—learn more about your company and the people who run it.

Remember: ***You will not be giving yourself a promotion this week****!*

The time designated for this section of the six-week program is allotted purely for you to hone your management skills without the pressures of the rigorous week-long promotion schedule, thus giving you ample time to stretch out and feel yourself fitting into your role as a manager. For some professionals the acquisition of good management skills is a lifelong process, one invested in learning the intricacies of human communication, understanding the value and reward of expertly administered conflict resolution methods and earning an appreciation for the broad applications of the psychology of group dynamics. Fortunately for you the *Faking Smart! Six-Week Program* doesn't dive too deep in all that theory. *You're a manager now... tighten your belt and start making some decisions!*

The Faking Smart! 12 Point Plan For Effective Business Management

Any Tom, Dick and Harry can tell how great their management scheme is, but it all comes down to how well it works in practice. Here are three accounts of *real* people who have used the *Faking Smart! 12 Point Plan For Effective Business Management* in real-world situations:

TOM SPINNER JR., CEO, WIDGET TECHNOLOGIES INC.

I attended an Ivy League school and graduated with a degree in pre-business. What I didn't expect after graduation was how difficult it would be to get a job. After jerking around for a couple of years and putting off my job-search, I read an article about the FSIHL master's degree program in one of the high-end business magazines. I figured... *What do I have to lose?* I had always held an interest in the widget industry. I knew from business and economics classes that demand for widgets was constant and I thought that it might be just the thing I could see myself getting involved in. But I didn't know the first thing about starting a company, managing it or what it would take to actually make a widget. Maybe, I thought, the FSIHL could help me focus and get me on track?

After four weeks at the FSIHL I came out a changed man. I had a completely different level of confidence and, on top of that, a model for my first real widget factory. (It was made of Popsicle sticks and it broke a couple of days later after my roommate came home drunk one night and tripped over it.)

Today, after finally reaching the later stages of product development, I can comfortably say that we have had nothing but fantastic success. Even before we located the future site for the factory, I was quick to implement the *Faking Smart! 12 Point Plan For Effective Business Management* and the results were phenomenal. Right now we are trying to lure the services of a famous Nigerian widget-maker to get the company on its feet. Once that has taken place, we see ourselves in full widget production by early next year. If it hadn't been for *Faking Smart!* none of this would have ever happened.

—Thanks to everyone at *Faking Smart!*

HAIL TO THE CHIEF! 67

DICK BEUFFOURT, VP OF STRATEGIC DEVELOPMENT, BRUSH-STROKE MARKETING

The 12 point plan is like adding oil to a well-oiled machine. By incorporating the *Faking Smart! 12 Point Plan For Effective Business Management* you get a powerful business tool fast without all the theory that weighs down other management plans. I should know. I incorporated the 12 point plan and the results were indisputable. After studying the pamphlets the FSRI provided on their system for nearly a week, I brought the 12 point plan right into use at a marketing research company that had recently hired me. In less than a month a roster of 78 part and full-time interviewers was reduced to only six. When my boss, an operations VP, came to check up on my progress, his jaw almost hit the floor. The next day he bumped me up to team-lead for a new marketing project. When I asked him why he had given me the promotion he smiled and said that they were outsourcing that whole division now.

To put it simply, the 12 point plan did all the work. Now, whenever I think about getting a new promotion, I go straight to the *Faking Smart!* rulebook.

—All my regards, KWA!

HARRY JANKOWSKOWITZ, MIDWEST PRESIDENT, SCHMERZ BREWERIES INC.

I was a low-level personnel manager when I first joined the Schmerz team. I stayed there for several years while the company saw its distribution slowly decline in the face of direct competition with larger breweries. After several lay-off measures the worst seemed inevitable: I was certain the company would be bankrupt unless the upper brass started to operate on a different business model. That's when I ran into an old friend who recommended that I take a month off of work and get a master's degree in *Faking Smart!* It all started to make sense!

When I got back to Schmerz, I really started to shake things up. Working from *Faking Smart!*'s "Belly-up" model I started by applying everything I learned at the FSIHL. Within four months our sales rocketed up - 148% and labor dropped to a quarter of what it had been. Within half a year we were on the front cover of *Fortune Finders Magazine*, where they called Schmerz Breweries one of the *"Top 25 companies to watch out for!"* Less than a year after having received my *Faking Smart!* master's degree, I was named president of Schmerz's strategic planning team.

Since then I've dropped beer from our product list and have put all our attention toward Moon Soup, an organic, vegan, oatmeal breakfast pudding. If there's a market for this, we'll find it!

—*Faking Smart!*, eh, I love you like a million bucks!

Without a doubt, the 12 point plan could be considered the perfect plan. Easy to implement, it is a drawback-free system that fits easily into any corporate environment.

As a future executive, it is critical to gain the respect you deserve from your peers and superiors. Using the *Faking Smart! 12 Point Plan* this process is broken down to 12 simple rules, all of which have been rigorously tested and approved by our FSRI research teams, military strategists, astronauts and actuaries. The plan has two main goals: first, to make you look like an effective manager; and second, to make you feel like one! The hard science has backed this up, now it's your turn to reap the rewards and go headlong into utilizing these basic principles. Designed like a delicately crafted corndog, our plan presents itself with a light, crispy exterior whose secret is revealed only after you add a dab of ketchup and sink your teeth into it! You have a *whole week* to practice these principals at your workplace. Good luck!

12 Points to Management Success!

1. Speak loudly—establish yourself as the person in charge. Everyone knows that the louder a person speaks the more authority he or she possesses. In your office and out on the center floor you should project yourself with the self-assuredness that comes with the territory. Like the drill sergeant in *Full Metal Jacket*, your voice should resonate throughout the building. If your office door is shut, make sure others can hear you ranting through the walls. When talking on the phone, make sure everyone else is able to tell what the conversation is about. Even when you are talking to yourself, speak loudly and with conviction! The volume of your voice, however, should not be misconstrued as anger. No. Tell somebody how good a job she is doing with a booming voice. Laugh with vigor. Flirt with gusto. A good manager can even whisper with a robust holler that lets everyone in on the secret!

2. Set unattainable goals. Just as a manager asserts his or her position by presenting a bold presence, he or she has to back up the bravado with the beef. Make the beef bold, and to do this we suggest you set at least one, if not more, unattainable goals for your floor employees to strive for each day. All business is dependent on quantifiable results. Stretching this premise to its limit offers an opportunity for unbounded results. See what your average floor team is doing in terms of productivity and then double or triple their production goal. If, during the day, your floor team averages 50 replies to customer questions, tell them during the morning briefing that you would like to see that number reach 150! This is exactly what they want—*a challenge!* There are many ways of setting impossible goals, so let your creative energies flow. If your goals are somehow met, however, resist the temptation to reward your team. You risk receiving too much attention from those above you and an escalation in unattainable goal-setting that may spin out of control.

3. Active listening–become a master at looking interested. Under normal circumstances you would tell someone who wants to talk to you to *bring it up with your assistant,* but there are times when you are cornered—unable to get away—and that's when knowing the skills of active listening can be invaluable. The FSRI has discovered that there are some basic rules to apply toward active listening. If someone insists upon talking directly to you, here is what you should do:

- **Look your narrator directly in the eye.** Stare at him or her and don't turn away or blink until he or she has stopped talking.
- **Take out a piece of chewing gum from your pocket, unwrap it slowly and then place the piece in your mouth.** Proceed to chew it loudly, preferably with smacking and popping sounds. If you feel generous, offer the other person a piece!
- **Get up close.** The closer you are to the person talking to you the better you show him or her that you are paying attention. An active listener will instigate gentle, physical contact, like putting

a hand on the other person's shoulder or rubbing his or her forearm. While doing this, always look concerned by nodding and humming.
- **Think about more important things.** While that person has your attention, go over (in your head) the things that are more important to you: *Did you get everything for the party you're having this weekend? What clothes will you wear tomorrow? Is it pasta tonight or chicken curry?* With a little practice active listening allows you to hit two birds with one stone!
- **Tears of sympathy.** Learning how to cry on cue is an invaluable skill. If the person in front of you is droning on and on and starting to make you sleepy, or if you find yourself incapable of feigning the slightest interest in what he or she is saying, welling your eyes up with tears is a powerful tool in making the impression that you care deeply for what is being said. There are many books at your local library or bookstore that can help you to learn how to cry, and self-help sections, particularly, are riddled with such books. *Some have even claimed that this book has enabled them to discover a latent talent for opening the floodgates of emotion.*
- **When a person is done talking to you, nod and look concerned.** Say this: *"I'm glad you brought that up. I'll get my assistant on it first thing."* Or you can smile and say, *"Boy, I'd hate to be in your shoes, but keep up the good work."* Whatever the case, making the impression that you stopped your busy schedule to hear that person speak their mind is worth a million dollars in earned loyalty. Whether or not you've acted on their comment or complaint is ultimately irrelevant.

There are many ways to practice active listening while away from work. Watching TV is one of the surest ways to exercise this skill. Another way is to ask your significant other how his or her day went, then use the methods described above!

4. Walk the talk and talk the walk. Simply put, the phrase *"Walk the talk…"* means that you should be walking and talking as much as possible. Business is done on the go today, and making the impression that you are constantly managing the latest crisis is essential to the *Faking Smart! 12 Point Plan*. If you can, walk with a cell phone in hand… even outside of the workplace! Walk while talking to a business colleague. Walk when you are telling an employee that you *no longer need her services*. Better yet, walk while texting someone that he's being fired! If you find yourself sitting down at your desk you will most likely discover that you aren't getting much done. **Get off your butt and walk!** The phrase, *"Talk the walk"* simply answers the question the first phrase implies: *"I'm talking,"* it says, *"and you can bet on it that I'm walking too!"* Walking is not only considered healthy, it also creates the image that you are on top of your game, guaranteeing the success of the company by showing how energetic and efficient you are by thinking on your feet!

5. The Five-Second Rule for decision making. Managers look best when they make split-decisions, therefore by making every decision you are presented with a five-second split-decision you earn respect and solidify your hold on power. "Yes" or "no" questions are obviously the easiest for a *Faking Smart!* manager to accommodate. If an employee asks if he can have a day off next week to get married, say *"no"* without hesitation. If someone comes up and wonders if a fellow employee in the cubicle next to him should be allowed to drink beer during work, give a quick and unqualified *"yes."* You've made the decision. Now let it stand. It doesn't matter what the consequences are, the fact that you've considered the problem and addressed it in a short order is all that counts.

Making split-decisions over open-ended questions, however, can be trickier fare. If, for example, an employee comes up to you and claims that a customer is concerned over appropriate federal compliance for licensing of a product, answer with an abrupt: *"Tell him to bring up his concerns with our licensing department at extension blah, blah, blah."* Likewise, if an employee comes up to you in tears and says that he just learned that his family pet has died, answer curtly with this: *"On behalf of myself and InCredidata (or whatever company you work for), we offer our condolences. Now get over it and show me some numbers!"* Remember, you have five seconds to come up with an answer to a problem or question. If your reply actually runs longer than it took to make the decision, don't worry. That the decision was resolved in five seconds is the crucial part. Business moves at a fast pace. By allowing yourself only five seconds to answer questions you are giving yourself time to fit in many more questions during the day. Imagine taking an hour to answer one single question. At that rate you would only answer eight questions in the day! (Six, if you deduct for a two-hour lunch.) By following the five-second rule you can answer 12 questions in a minute, 720 questions in an hour or 4320 questions in a full, 24 hour day! No wonder split-second decision makers are the ones that make it to the top. With the five-second rule you also avoid the pitfall most managers find themselves in: over-thinking the over-thinkable. *"Don't over-think it,"* reminds the FSRI. *"Make it a split-decision and git'r done!"*

6. Multi multi-task it! If you can't multi-task today, you probably won't be hired as a manager at a competitive, cutting-edge company. The top human resource departments in the country are on the hunt for active multi-taskers; therefore, proving to your co-workers and higher-ups that you are a task-mastering multi-tasker is an excellent way to portray yourself as a manager willing to go the distance when it comes to helping with the company's success. With this in mind, the FSRI took it upon itself to bring multi-tasking under the microscope of intense *Faking Smart!* investigation, and what we discovered was mind-numbing. After countless experiments and clinical trials our research team learned that by simply increasing the number of things a manager did while multi-tasking, that person turned out to be 74% more likely to get a promotion. In other words, the more things one does simultaneously, the more likely that person is to become a VP! We termed this new idea *multi* multi-tasking, and have included it as one of the groundbreaking theories in the 12 Point Plan you are currently skimming through. Simply put, seven out of ten managers that practiced the new *multi* multi-tasking strategy were given promotions at their company or firm *way ahead* of those who stuck to regular old multi-tasking. To incorporate this strategy into your 12 Point Plan, begin by multi-tasking and then go from there. If, while you review a pair of entry level staff résumés, you can also go over yesterday's numbers, and at the same time look at the company's long term strategies report for the next quarter, you are demonstrating basic multi-tasking skills. Now, take this a step further: *add a few more things to the list.* By doing so, you transform yourself from a run-of-the-mill multi-tasker to the exceptional rank of *multi* multi-tasker! Along with performing the activities mentioned above, add at least four or more of the following activities (optimally, you should be able to manage at least seven tasks at once):

1. Juggle something, like apples or paperweights. (Any combination will work.)
2. Lift arm or leg weights, or practice aerobics in your office.
3. Pace back and forth.
4. Practice crying.
5. Type furiously on your keyboard on a topic of your choice.
6. Shout with blind rage at something that just came up on your computer.
7. Make a copy of your résumé and have your assistant send it to a company you are interested in working for. Then, before it's sent, decide against it on ethical grounds.
8. Take a call from an operations VP.
9. Call up someone in Strategic Planning and drop some brilliant idea of yours (…if you don't come up with a brilliant idea tell the exec that you'll call him back when you remember what it was. The fact that you *had* an idea makes a good impression).
10. Stick a three-day-old fish in the employee break room refrigerator.
11. Have your assistant put together a birthday card for your father, then "realize" that it isn't his birthday.
12. Befriend a floor employee.
13. Fire a floor employee.

14. Draw up a plan.
15. Have your assistant attempt to *multi* multi-task (if you are both *multi* multi-tasking, the impression you make is unforgettable!)

If you feel comfortable, by all means, do all these things at the same time. *Multi* multi-taskers show that they can go above and beyond what is expected of them and thus set the precedent for what should be seen in an up-and-coming executive!

7. Play the blame game. Being blamed for some wrongdoing is an everyday occurrence at most companies. In these places of work blame goes around like a virus during the flu season; sooner or later it will find its way to you. That's why you have to protect your image by becoming a preemptive master at playing the blame game and learn to spread blame quickly and evenly for the optimal results. If, for example, the "higher-ups" are complaining about not receiving a weekly report, blame your computer for not attaching the document to your email. If an account manager starts whining about your low numbers, blame it on a lazy floor staff and release ten employees. If other office workers in the building are concerned about how fistfights have spilled out from your floor and into the company halls, point your finger at Hollywood and blame the movies for the ugly rise in our culture of violence.

See, you've directed attention away from where blame naturally falls and allowed yourself the time to react in an appropriate corporate manner. *"When you feel like you are being blamed,"* asserts the FSRI, *"blame back!"*

Another way of responding to criticism or concern is to blame the person blaming you for playing the blame game! When blame is used in this way, you direct blame right back at the blamer. This renders their argument ineffective and you come out looking sharper for having stood your ground.

As you increase your proficiency in playing the blame game, you'll come to realize that blame can be scattered around in nearly every occasion. You will find that you can blame someone for blaming someone else. You can place blame on inanimate objects such as doors, floors or chairs. You can even place blame on animals for not being smart! When you utilize blaming, you avoid the uncomfortable process of self-examination and allow yourself to put your time and energy toward more important things.

Whatever you do, though, do not cast blame upon yourself. Sure, once in a while it's fun to blame yourself for something when out at a bar or when you are among friends, but when at work be careful of this treacherous self-entangling web. Self-blame can lead quickly to a downward slide of self-esteem which is much more difficult to deal with than blaming someone else for your faults. Lastly, never blame the *Faking Smart! Six Week Program*, the FSRI or the FSIHL for anything that might go wrong during your experience with any of the *Faking Smart!* schemes, projects or plans. Yes, blame is necessary and effective at your place of work, but when you place blame on *Faking Smart!* you have taken the blame game too far!

8. Become a mentor. It is an unspoken rule in big business today that a wise executive nurtures and trains a protégé to take the executive's place in the event of that executive's promotion or departure. This training guarantees that the life and personality of the executive lives on in the protégé, so that the cycle can repeat itself when the protégé then becomes executive and in turn finds a new protégé herself. The same cycle holds true for the manager/entry-level employee relationship. By selecting a protégé, the manager insures that, after she has been promoted, a solid and admiring person is in line for her position.

There is only *one* condition that should be placed on selecting an ideal protégé, and this condition is grounded in two factors. First, the protégé should be of the same sex as the manager. This helps to avoid applying the label of "super-pet" to what is, in actuality, a protégé. (If the manager is gay, the protégé should then, of course, be of the opposite sex, although in certain industries and sections of the country, this rule may be reversed.) Second, the protégé should resemble you in appearance, if possible. This helps to remind you that, when working with your protégé, you are actually working to improve your own image and rank. By "looking in the mirror," you remind yourself that you are taking care of number one! When you have selected your protégé, take her out to lunch and impart to her all of your wisdom and knowledge. At the end of lunch ask her if there are any questions she might have, then head back to the office and present your new protégé to the floor staff in a brief protégé-christening ceremony. **Congratulations, you've just created a protégé!** Now you can get your promotion without worrying that competition for your job will involve a petty, bare-knuckle squabble between a manager's pets and super-pets. **Your protégé will now carry the torch!**

9. Advice from your old boss–priceless. One of the best-kept secrets in corporate management is the usefulness of plumbing the knowledge of your predecessor for advice and guidance. Sure, you may have ousted your old manager in an ugly, quasi-Machiavellian coup, and this may lead you to believe that she might detest and resent you and never want to hear your voice again. Not true! Managers, like most people, have one thing in common: they love attention. Calling your old manager up to ask advice on how to use the break-room coffee-maker, or whether the "F" files in the file drawer were placed before or after the "G" files, is a great way of helping her get over her sour grapes. Whether you need her advice or not, giving your old boss a call *just to say hello* is a great way of suggesting that you have *her* to thank for all the success you are currently having while also giving *you* a chance to update her on the new strategies and tactics you are now implementing to get things back on track. She'll also be curious to learn how everything is going regarding the old floor staff: who's dating whom, who won the last production award and who is sleeping with her old super-pet? Be sure to tell her how much more money you make than she did and that everything is running smoothly. This will put her at ease and make her feel better for having left. In the end you will have made, perhaps, a lifelong friend whom you can consult when you run into trouble or when you just don't feel like talking to anybody else.

A word of caution: remind her that her appearance at the company will *still* result in an arrest. Also, if you plan on having lunch with your old boss, make sure you have one of the company body guards or Enforcer robots to escort you… just in case any latent friction surfaces during your innocent tête á tête.

10. Move someone's cheese. There has been so much discussion lately on the theory of moving someone's cheese that the FSRI has decided it is worth including in the *Faking Smart! 12 Point Plan*.

The practice of moving someone's cheese is as old as cheese itself, and incorporating this ancient ritual into your management plan is essential to your becoming a better and more efficient leader. Breakrooms are full of all kinds of opportunities for moving cheese around. You can move cheese from someone's sandwich. You can give out cheese and then, when someone has gone to the bathroom or is otherwise occupied, move the cheese you just gave him! The disadvantage to moving a lot of cheese, simply put, is that cheese is sometimes smelly and oily, and this odor can get under your fingernails and get smeared into your clothes. So *be careful* when moving cheese around. In addition, with the recent rise of cheeses imported from France, Holland and Greece, cheeses have become extremely watery and crumbly. Getting your hands around a clump of one of these "non-native" cheeses is risky business, and you may find yourself making an embarrassing goof-up when an employee catches you in the act of attempting to move a heap of mushy Feta, your fingers and hands smothered with this exotic, yet pungent amalgam of soured goat's milk and curd. The FSRI recommends sticking to a simple hunk of cheddar, if at all possible.

Yes, the practice of moving cheese is well known and respected in today's office environment, and by getting your fingers in the pot you help to secure your reputation as a stand-out leader! (For the sake of brevity, cottage cheese and cream cheese have been excluded from our plan. These cheeses come in easy to carry, recyclable plastic tubs and don't require the same skill and stealth in moving as other cheeses.)

11. Do office stuff. When you can't think of anything else to do, or when you are too tired or disinterested to implement any of the other points in the 12 point plan, doing office stuff is a great way of making yourself look like a busy, overworked manager. Doing office stuff is composed of an array of differing tasks and diversions. Doing any of this stuff is a great way of passing the time while you keep up the appearance that you are focused and on task. Here is a brief list of stuff you can do in your office:

1. Scan old databases and assemble random reports.
2. Set up a deadline for a project with a code name, then have your
    assistant feel your terror whenever you mention this code name, your

eyes alit with panic and fear.
3. Perform employee reviews that go on for several days.
4. Perform reviews of those employee reviews.
5. Update the operating system on your computer only to lose everything you had on your hard-drive.
6. Spend the rest of the week with the tech-support guy trying to dig up the critical data you lost during the operation system update.
7. Don't practice putting into a plastic cup... this is a shallow stereotype that doesn't apply to lower level management. It is a valid stereotype, however, for more senior execs at the company (...so you might want to save this kind of "stuff" for later).
8. Set out a candy jar at the end of your desk with a sign that says "Take ONE if you think you deserve it."
9. Re-fill your pens with fresh ink.
10. Put your feet up on your desk, lean back and have a serious conversation.

The benefit of learning how to do different office things shows in the quality of your work appearance. Again, be creative and let your juices flow. The office stuff you have at your disposal is infinite, and familiarizing yourself with the ease at which office stuff can be done is a great way to secure the image of an effective manager with an impressive personal agenda.

Woot, Woot!

So there you have it, the *Faking Smart! 12 Point Plan* covers everything a manager in the *Faking Smart! Six-Week Program* will ever need to know! As a comprehensive scheme, the 12 point plan should provide the new manager with the skills and visual strength needed to appear professional and in charge, and *that*, according to the research at the FSRI, is all that matters. Be liberal this week when employing any of the 12 points at your place of work, and practice them to the point of exhaustion if at all possible. Remember, each of the points listed above has been thoroughly studied and put to the test, so don't be afraid to incorporate them in your daily routine. Good luck! We are with you to the end of the program where you'll revel in the knowledge that you've reached the *Faking Smart!* expectation of becoming a genuine and steadfast VP!

[A word from the FSRI Division of Lists: You may have become aware that the *Faking Smart! 12 Point Plan,* at present, consists of only eleven points. We apologize for this inconvenience. In the haste to put together this revolutionary scheme it became apparent, only after the book had gone to print, that the author, under the extreme pressures and deadlines imposed by his publisher, had forgotten to include the 12th and critical, final point. Please, do not lose sleep over this. Since the discovery of this shortfall the author and the FSRI have been working around the clock, devoting all their energy and resources to come up with the final point, and when it is tested and complete it will be published at its soonest availability. Again, we are sorry if this lapse has caused any undue difficulties in your ability to fake smart, but we encourage you, in no way, to consider our 12 point plan unusable or incomplete. 11 Points is a pretty darn good deal when you consider it. It beats the heck out of any eight point plan, and still outdoes a ten point plan by a point. In fact, we suggest that, until the 12th point is published that you go ahead and feel comfortable using the 12 point plan as if it were a valid and whole 12 point plan. As it currently stands, the author and the FSRI will readily vouch for the effectiveness of the "nearly" finished 12 point plan and challenge any who might find it in their nature to disagree.]

Your Week at a Glance

Along with your implementation of the 12 point plan, there are a few important things you should accomplish during your third week on the job. When you have the time, stroll around your building and get to know where the executives are. Take a latte with you, and when you bump into an executive offer him or her a sip from your cup. Introduce yourself with an "InCredidata smile" and toss your head back and laugh casually at anything that is said. As a manager you're part of the upper crust now, and your behavior speaks a thousand words. If you pop your head in an office and you see that Sam Kilbert has a trophy case full of golf awards, tell him that you still love Tiger Woods and think he'll win an Emmy this year. If, when you poke your face into Susan Champion's office, you notice that she surrounds herself with beautiful plants, tell her that you that you secretly wish every woman executive was given a glass ceiling! Whatever you do, just be yourself. You're *Faking Smart!* and have the benefit of huge amounts of time and research backing your every move. When you return to your desk, jot down the names of everyone who was at least a President of Operations or higher. On Monday this list will be the critical element for making Week Four a success.

In the meantime, have fun developing your 12 point plan. Try to come to your office late and be out early each day and get all the work out of your assistant that you pay him to do. If you can, provide your protégé with a schedule of the "look" you will be incorporating from Monday to Friday and tell her to wear the exact same thing you'll be wearing. This gives other employees a sense of your organizational synchronicity and will help to remind them who will get your job when you move on next week.

Yes! Keep your eye on becoming a new member of the operations team in the next chapter where *Faking Smart!* guides you through the ABC's of becoming a winning corporate fit! When you become an operations team member your job begins to take a more serious turn… one where all conventional rules of doing business are out the window!

Week 4
BRING ON THE CLOWNS

SO, YOU'VE SAILED THROUGH WEEK THREE with hardly any effort whatsoever. Fantastic! By following the tenets of our *Faking Smart! Six-Week Program* you've skillfully slipped into your management chair, earned the trust and respect of your new subordinates and, through an intense study and implementation of the *Faking Smart!* 12 Point Plan to Successful Business Management, you've taken corporate management to a level never before imagined! Like a boat adrift in high seas, you are steadily moving toward our ultimate goal—*making you a VP!*

Week Four Run-Down

In Week Four we return to our weekly promotion schedule. By Friday you will have waved goodbye to your manager's office, protégé, floor personnel and the *12 Point Plan*. Get ready, because this week finds you re-introduced to the company as corporate wunderkind and newest member of the operations team!

QUESTION: *WHAT IF I LIKE BEING A MANAGER AND WANT TO REMAIN ONE?*

We pose this question merely because many participants in the *Six-Week Program,* at this point, have a tendency to ask it. The answer is simple: sure, it might be nice to be a manager, but you only have three weeks left before you become a VP. *Why stop now?* Three weeks may seem like a long way off, but with the power of the FSRI and the full force of the *Faking Smart! Six-Week Program* behind you, getting the corner office and the leverage of having *unlimited horizontal job potential* will seem like a walk in the park! Don't sweat it. You can do it! We know that we think you can!

QUESTION: *WHY DO I HAVE TO READ SO MUCH JUST TO BECOME A VP?*

The FSRI, FSIHL and your humble author have all wondered why we have to write so much just to get someone like you to the coveted title of VP. Couldn't we just compress the entire program into a ten minute YouTube video, it has been asked? Yes, we could compress it to a ten minute YouTube video... but then how would we sell any books?

The truth is, after extensive studies, many of which have involved blindfolds, environments, impacts and clinics, we have come to a solid and irrefutable conclusion regarding the effects reading this book has on nearly all six-week program participants. Research done in the bowels of the FSRI have shown that the chances a six-week program participant has of finishing the six-week program are actually multiplied in direct relation to the number of books that participant owns! For example, if a six-week program participant buys and owns five copies of this book, the chances of that person completing the six-week program are FIVE times greater than if that person owned only one copy of the book. *"Facts are facts,"* as we say it at the FSRI. It may be hard to believe, but you can't argue against *Faking Smart!*

Back to *Faking Smart!* and Week Four!

So, you're raring to get to work and to dive into Week Four! Great, glad you are here! This week there are three things you need to do to successfully complete this part of the program: first, you will be required to orchestrate a worker revolt; second, you will exercise crisis management skills to win your position on the operations team; finally, you will have to pull off the behavior and "fit" that proves to the operations team that you are definitely the wunderkind they have come to expect!

Your Floor Team is Your Power Base

You may not realize it, but at this point in the six-week program you've amassed a devoted and enthusiastic power base: your own floor staff! Yes! By exercising the 12 point plan in the previous week you've demonstrated that you're a one-in-a-million manager—the kind rarely seen wandering the halls of corporate America today—and you've dazzled your team by implementing some of the most cutting edge techniques known to business! You've nurtured a protégé, shown yourself to be an expert listener and multi multi-tasking decision-maker and you've proven to everyone that you aren't afraid to throw yourself into a dirty round of the blame game when circumstances warrant. Yes, you can walk the talk… and they know it! Your floor team has become your loyal power base—a power base you now can tap to catapult you up the corporate ladder to your next promotion!

Monday

Try getting in to work a little earlier today for a fresh start, at least a half-hour before noon to ensure you won't be late for lunch. When you return from lunch have your assistant type up this "official" office memo:

INCREDIDATA MEMO

ATTN: (your name here)

Due to current economic exigencies, the operations team, after cursory review, has concluded that a number of services provided to your floor personnel will be either reduced or fully eliminated. Effective tomorrow:

- **No more heating will be provided to the service center floor. Encourage employees to dress in layers (wool is most effective), wear hats and to take a quick lap around the office if an increase body temperature is necessary.**
- **To conserve on electricity and water usage, bathrooms will be off limits to floor personnel. For this to work, discourage the drinking of beverages during office hours—especially coffee! (In fact we recommend a complete ban of coffee on the floor to help accommodate this change.) If an employee absolutely needs to use the toilet, suggest that he or she use a peanut butter jar or use allotted break time to leave the building and seek a public facility nearby.**

- All water coolers will be converted to recycled water coolers. The bottoms of the cooler bottles will be cut open to allow water not completely consumed by personnel to be re-added to the existing bottle.
- All lights (excluding the manager's office lights) will be turned off during business hours. Personnel will be required to bring a flashlight or battery powered lantern, or other suitable, approved lighting apparatuses to their workstations. Overhead lighting will be provided ten minutes before opening and ten minutes before closing, to illuminate walkways and to ensure employees enter and exit safely.
- All employees will be required to purchase and utilize their own computer systems. IT will assist in setting up and connecting these systems with the company-wide network. If, however, an external computer has been connected with the internal company network, this computer must remain on InCredidata grounds. This policy is a security measure to avoid accidental intelligence leaks to outside interests.
- Printers will be disconnected and disabled. Insist that, from now on, all copies will be hand written.
- All stock office materials, i.e. pens, paper, paperclips etc... must be purchased and provided by personnel. Any existing stock will be removed and donated to the humane society.
- The break room will be locked and off limits during business hours. Its purpose will be reserved exclusively for employee interrogations.

We know these may be considered stringent restrictions on your InCredidata staff, but these measures are put in place to comply with the broader belt-tightening InCredidata must implement in order to remain viable in today's competitive business environment.

Thanks, Operations

P.S. Be sure to get your name in for the InCredidata penthouse hotel raffle for our bi-annual, week-long, corporate Hawaiian retreat! And yes (as promised) massages, polo, whale-watching cruises and professional golf lessons will be available free this year to all managers and executives! Hang loose and aloha!!

Have your assistant print four or five copies of this memo and disperse them in visible locations around the worker floor, then call your protégé in for a meeting. When your protégé arrives, explain your surprise and remorse that this confidential memo found it's way into the hands of the floor staff. Then indicate your deep sympathy and describe your intention to curtail these drastic cuts. Express to your protégé that the only possible way to avoid this mess is if *you* get promoted to the operations team where you can serve the interests of your floor personnel and make sure budget-trimming measures are diverted to other, more deserving departments… *such as IT support where they do nothing but sit around all day, ignoring calls and playing computer games.* Notify your protégé that the Operations Department is coming down at 3:30 p.m. to visit the floor to make sure these new rules are being implemented and that your protégé's job will be to write a formal letter of protest (signed by all floor staff) which he or she will present during the meeting. (*It just so happens that you have already composed this announcement for your protégé!*) It runs as follows:

To Operations:

We, as floor staff in the service center of InCredidata, are united in our opposition to your latest attempts to impose extreme restrictions on our ability to perform basic work activities.

> *It is beneath the dignity of every employee here, or, for that matter, any employee of InCredidata, to comply with such outrageous and draconian demands. In fact, a basic review of state labor law and the Geneva Workers Convention would suggest that the measures being imposed may constitute criminal activity.*
>
> *We are tired of being treated as the invisible employees of InCredidata, and resent any attempt to further demean or degrade us.*
>
> **Signed, the Floor Staff**

Hand this script to your protégé and indicate that he or she should wait for your cue to read this during the meeting.

Next up, tell your assistant to call maintenance and schedule a power down for all of your floor computer systems for a "Homeland Security drill" from 3:30 to 3:45 today. (This guarantees that you will have the full attention of your floor staff just when you need it.) Then have your assistant prepare and send this email to all upper management and InCredidata executives (the people you've met during your office tours):

> **Come one, come all!**
>
> *Show support for your InCredidata call center by joining us for a short celebration of floor team cost-cutting initiatives!*
>
> *In light of a challenging business climate, your call center floor team has taken a pro-active approach to helping InCredidata to be more productive and more competitive. Join us at 3:30 pm sharp today to see InCredidata spirit at its best!*
>
> *And bring a treat to share!*

Finally, prepare the two letters you will need when these two groups have their run-in. The first letter is a notice of your resignation as floor manager (...make this brief and to the point.) The second letter is one that notifies upper management, specifically an operations VP, of your humble intent to accept a promotion to the operations team. Now, collect all your things in a box—tell your assistant to do likewise—print out the letters and update your blog or Twitter page until three o'clock rolls around, then go get yourself a latte and time it so that you make it back to the office before these groups get better acquainted!

Creating Opportunity Out of Crisis

Everyone knows that leaders are born out of crisis. This is one of the oldest pieces of wisdom known to mankind. That's why today is the perfect opportunity for you to take advantage of the crisis you've created to show the upper brass just what kind of leader you can be. When two groups of people with differing perspectives are forced together in one room, conflict between these groups is inevitable. Knowing exactly why these two groups of people are meeting and why they may be concerned or upset stands to your advantage. By taking control of the situation—by stepping in to mediate—you demonstrate a profound ability to resolve conflict and rise above the ground level fray. You become the master of the situation. By *thinking quickly on your feet* you divert potential disaster... and you create an indelible impression on the people responsible for giving you your next promotion!

Zero Hour

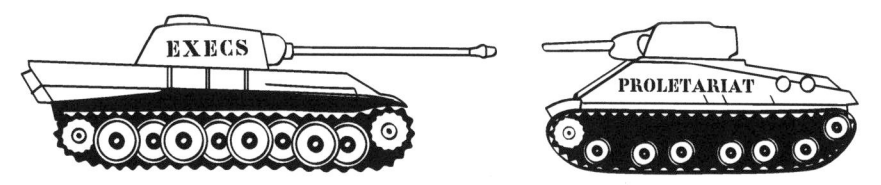

You've got your latte in hand, you're strutting down the hall to enter your floor staff room and you can smell the scent of poly-knit Teflon carpet and can hear it as it crinkles under your feet. You've got what it takes! You've been following every detail of the *Faking Smart! Six-Week Program*, so there can be no reason for you to throw your hands up and flee the building in panic and fear.

You look good. You feel good! We know it! It's 3:29. Get out your cell phone and place a call to your mechanic and demand to know when your SAAB will be out of the shop. As you push open the door and elbow your way past upper managers and executives, raise your voice and say into the phone: *"I don't care what it takes. Just get it done. Do you hear me? Just get it done!"* Then turn off your phone, roll your eyes and take a long sip from your latte. Cue your protégé with a wink and then retreat to your office. As planned, the computers are down and everyone in the room is standing around like curious prairie dogs. Your protégé then begins to read from the open letter of protest and, word by word, tensions in the room escalate. Slowly, but surely, a chant begins to build from the floor personnel: *No more cuts, no more cuts…* The management and executives bristle with apprehension and confusion (they expected a party, after all). *"How can this be happening,"* they start to think. *"Something's definitely not right here. This could get dangerous."* Now, just before tempers begin to boil over and before injury-causing objects find their mark, gather yourself, exit your office and intervene. With your latte raised high, state in a commanding voice: **ENOUGH!** Wait for everyone's attention, then make this announcement:

> **I want everyone here to take a deep breath and calm down. We all know that there are differences of opinion in this room, and that there are people on both sides that feel that they haven't been given a chance to be heard. But before things get out of control, I want all present to understand that we, as InCredidata employees, are bigger than this. We are in this together and only together can we work this out. Now, I've taken some time to weigh my options here and I think I've come up with a solution that all parties can feel good about, and I'll lay out the specifics in a moment.**
>
> **TO THE FLOOR PERSONNEL: To my personnel—I want to say this: In all the time we've spent together you've taught me more than you could ever imagine. You've given me strength, courage and a desire to meet**

deadlines and exceed client expectations on nearly every project that has come my way. It is to you that I owe the fact that I am possibly the best manager InCredidata has ever had working for them. Tom, Brittany, Sam *(these are common names, and there is a high likelihood that there is a Tom, Brittany and Sam among your floor staff.)* I want to thank you specifically for your hard work and devotion. You've kept the numbers up, represented InCredidata with energy and optimism, and you exemplify, as do I, what InCredidata holds highest—spirit, productivity and pride. Thank you.

To make this short, I've come to the conclusion that there is only one solution to resolving this current impasse, and that is for me to immediately resign my position as floor manager (yes, it's true) and to accept a *new* position on the operations team! To all my floor personnel, I give you my gratitude. To my new office and employers, I am honored to accept this promotion, and I guarantee—*you will not be disappointed! Now let's get back to work InCredidata!*

As the cheers erupt from your floor staff (they will be extremely excited to hear that you're leaving), have your assistant deliver your letters of both resignation and acceptance to the most senior operations executive present, then signal your assistant to notify maintenance to power up the computers and to tell you protégé that the management job is all hers. Don't be shy... ask an executive right away where your new office is located and then have your assistant follow you up to your new floor and your new job with the operations team!

Your New Rung on the Corporate Ladder!

Congratulations! You've made it one more step up the rung to corporate success! With only a few clever sleights of hand you've proven to your company and to yourself that you have what it takes to make it in corporate America. You're four weeks into the six-week program, and with only two weeks to go, you may not realize it, but you're looking and acting more and more like a VP with every day that passes!

Like a fledgling eaglet peering out from its nest atop a 150 foot dead Douglas fir tree teetering precariously on the edge of a rocky cliff, we're here to give you that final push... to watch you as your wings open and you are buffeted by the wind, and as you soar upward toward your final goal—*becoming a VP!*

A Brief Word From the FSRI

While there is little or no statistical evidence that a participant in the *Six-Week Program* will fail to achieve the results described in Monday's schedule, the FSRI has decided to make it known that in some isolated instances—instances where the specific Week Four details were overlooked or simply left out—there are reports of unexpected outcomes. While presumably fictional in nature, one account has a past six-week program participant finding herself immediately promoted to President of Operations after displaying heroism during this disastrous inner-company imbroglio. In a heartbeat she was denied everything she had worked so hard to achieve in the six-week program—she would never see her name with a "VP" next to it—and has since lapsed into a deep and irretrievable depression... albeit, still working as a functional operations president.

Another case drummed up and reported to the FSRI through backdoor channels recalls the plight of one unlucky participant who, after the presentation of his speech, was tackled to the ground and immobilized by staff robots. This same report placed him as physically impaired to this day with a case against the robot manufacturers still pending in state superior court. The last cautionary tale comes from an undisclosed western state where a full-blown riot ensued between upper management and floor personnel. Our poor manager, in this story, was caught in the middle of this petty, self-serving melee and has never been heard from since.

Do not fret! As mentioned, these accounts are anecdotal and should in no way be considered factual or true. What is true, however, is that hundreds, if not, thousands of tests have been performed by the FSRI in labs with trained and certified *Faking Smart!* actors, extras and technicians, and in nearly every case the six-week program participant in this portion of the program received the promotion we set as a goal. Remember, you're not alone. *Faking Smart!* is with you every step of the way... free-climbing along with you up that crumbling, icy mountain face, coaxing you on till your VP flag is planted firmly on the summit!

Tuesday

So there's a lot of tension going around the company since this last near disastrous clash between upper management and your floor personnel. While you may hold that bygones be bygones, when you come in to work on Tuesday there's sure to be a degree of tension among your new coworkers. In addition, you may unknowingly elicit some feelings of envy and jealousy among the members of the operations team... creating the kind of anxiety and mistrust all such teams experience when a new wunderkind plops down in their midst. Not to worry! In this stage of the *Faking Smart! Six-Week Program* we lighten things up a bit and allow you to express yourself with some good old fashioned theatrics!

Zwango the Corporate Clown!

It's true... everyone loves a clown, and today you'll have opportunity to do just what you've always dreamed of doing: **brightening up your office with laughter and cheer!** This Tuesday you'll adopt the moniker of "Zwango, the Corporate Clown", the rib-tickling prankster that everyone in the office will come to love and adore. With each gag that Zwango pulls from his bag of tricks, watch how coworker stress evaporates and the mood becomes one of shared jubilation and merriment!

THINGS TO TAKE WITH YOU ON TUESDAY:
1. Clown outfit with makeup, large red nose, red wig and oversized shoes
2. Pillowcase
3. Silly string
4. Balloon-tying balloons
5. Rubber chicken
6. Slide whistle
7. Hand held bicycle horn
8. Lapel flower with remote squirter
9. Puppy
10. Trick, compactable flower bouquet

When you come into work on Tuesday, come on time—say ten or so—and dressed up in your *full Zwango costume*. When your assistant shows you to your new desk (she'll already have your work station set up for you) lug your pillow case full of gags to your chair and act surprised and delighted (and professional). Then commence with dusting off the imaginary bits of dust and dirt from your seat. Pick up a piece of this imaginary dust, examine it and then throw it over your shoulder. Once your chair is "clean", sit down in a formal manner, stretch out your arms and then smooth out your clown suit with a meticulous and systematic, self-conscious preening. When this is done, loosen the collar at your neck, silently crack your knuckles and then flutter your fingertips as if you were a concert pianist ready to tackle a Rachmaninov piano concerto. Then, out of nowhere, drop your jaw and stare blankly at the computer in front of you! Pick up your keyboard and explore this strange device. Stand up on your seat and crawl up on your desk to get a look behind the computer screen. Once on your desk, stand up and actually walk around the computer as if it were some strange alien object—a piece of outlandish and baffling technology.

At this point your assistant joins in the fun!

Have your assistant come over to your desk and ask if you need any help. (Set this up before hand.) Give a honk—one honk signifying a "yes"—from your horn and nod. Pout and pretend to rub your eyes as if crying. When your assistant powers up your computer act elated and jump around with joy. Jump down on the floor and run around in circles while you honk your horn. Pretend to rub your eyes now... *with tears of happiness!* Give a coworker a hug. Sit in a coworker's lap and run your fingers through his or her hair. Then run back to your desk, sit down and then promptly pretend to fall asleep. Snore loudly! After two minutes or so, jump up as if awakened from a dream. Yawn and then set your self to typing at a prodigious pace. Hammer thousands of characters down in a furious burst of inspiration... in fact, type on your keyboard so furiously that you fall off your chair! Your assistant comes to the rescue once more. *"I think it's time Zwango takes a short break,"* she says to the growing ranks of onlookers. Give a single "honk" for yes, pick up your pillowcase and start your tour of the new office area!

Zwango Tours the Office

So, you've established the good times Zwango will bring to the office today. Rumor will spread quickly, so get around and meet everyone before the novelty of your outfit wears thin and loses the element of surprise. Have your assistant lead you around the office, from door to door to various executives and project managers' offices. When introduced to a particularly attractive executive, Zwango will undoubtedly blush with shy affection. But Zwango isn't so humble that he or she won't use this opportunity to practice a bit of formal office flirtation. With decorum and deference, reach down into your pillowcase and pull out the bouquet of flowers—VOILA!—and now it's the executive's turn to blush with embarrassed appreciation! If the executive asks if you have ever been forcibly housed in an asylum, play along with the gag and nod and give a single "HONK". When your assistant corrects you, roll your eyes and produce a woeful "HONK, HONK", meaning the negative or "no". Then it's on to the next important person among your office personnel! Feel free to use your lapel squirter and slide whistle when occasion calls for it... and save the puppy sleeping at the bottom of your pillowcase as a special gift to the operations president!

If, during the course of the day, someone decides to pose a direct question to you—one that warrants more then a simple "yes" or "no" honk—have your assistant make it clear that Zwango is so humble and modest that he or she only feels comfortable communicating with his or her assistant. If, for example, one of your team members comes up and is rude enough to ask if Zwango is "unbalanced" and advises that Zwango quickly lose the clown getup, respond by whispering something quickly into your assistant's ear. She then relates what you've told her: *"Zwango says that, yes, he is balanced. He just rode his unicycle to work this morning, and that laughter is good for the soul and a fundamental part of a constructive, professional environment."* Then squirt him with your lapel flower and make a ruckus with your horn while running in tight circles!

After you've made your rounds and met the important people on your new office floor, go back to your desk, crawl under it and take a nap. After some time has passed, emerge and yawn and stretch out your arms and legs. Then hike up the belt of your clown suit (have your assistant accompany this act by making a quick tone with your slide whistle) and casually saunter over to the water cooler. Closely examine this odd contraption—tap at it and watch the bubbles move around in the refreshing, cool inaccessible liquid floating inside the large blue bottle. Observe your hand as it is grows large and ungainly when placed on the opposite side. Stand up and then lean casually against the cooler as you check your watch and give a deferential nod to the coworker that passes by. Then carefully tilt the bottle on its stand. Kick the stand a few times and then lasciviously lick the blue bottle to see if you can get any of the water out. At this point have your assistant come over and nonchalantly fill her cup up at the spigot and then return to her desk. (Set this up beforehand.) Zwango can't believe it! Zwango plays with the spigot and watches the water pour out with fascinated amusement. Keep the nozzle held down and then kneel on the floor and try to catch some of it in your mouth! It's not working too well… most of the water is winding up on your face and on the floor! Now things start getting really messy! You've created a small puddle of water at the base of the cooler and your attempts to quench your thirst have created pandemonium! You slip, you slide… at last the bottle comes tumbling down and everyone in the office is roaring with laughter! You're soaked. You've created a happy and memorable mood among your new coworkers, upper management and execs! But now that Zwango is soaked from head to toe, it's time for him to say goodbye to all the great people he's met today!

As your assistant escorts you toward the elevator, don't be surprised if you are accosted by well-wishers and others thanking you for brightening up their day. *"Bye, Zwango!,"* they'll shout. *"We love you!"* Now cry a few crocodile tears, wave and whisper into your assistant's ear. *"Zwango says he loves everyone and that if you want to come visit him at his pony farm you are welcome any time!"* HONK, HONK, HONK, HONK!

Tuesday's Recap

While slightly unconventional, Zwango has made everyone breathe a little bit easier today, and you can rest assured that tensions in the office are greatly reduced due to your willingness to introduce the gift of laughter to your workplace. You may not realize it, but you've gained street cred today. You're creative, daring and good-natured, and believe it or not, this is all the office will be talking about for some time to come. Sure, you might have ruffled a few feathers by introducing your coworkers to Zwango—there are always a few party-poopers who simply reject the idea of fun—but the dividends will come to outweigh any negative side-effects. Now go home and get a good night's sleep. You've got plenty to do on Wednesday and you need to stay sharp for your final Week Four tactic of the *Faking Smart! Six-Week Program!*

Attend a Conference

Without question, any self-respecting corporate employee has attended a conference or two during his or her quick ascendancy on a corporate ladder. Horror stories of hazardous travel to distant seminars are part and parcel in today's corporate experience, so Wednesday is your perfect opportunity to stick one more plume into your increasingly feathered corporate hat!

THINGS TO HAVE WITH YOU WEDNESDAY BEFORE ARRIVING AT WORK:

1. A travel bag with a two days change of clothes
2. A cell phone
3. Laptop computer
4. $1500 cash
5. A travel pillow and one bottle of Dramamine

Wednesday to Friday – *Viva Las Vegas!*

You've got a colossal amount of work ahead of you today, so make it in to the office as early as possible—say, somewhere between ten and eleven. When you arrive, greet your assistant in your typical harried and frazzled manner and tell her to buy a business class ticket for a flight that afternoon to Las Vegas and to reserve a room at an upscale Las Vegas airport hotel. Once she secures the flight and hotel accommodations, go quickly over the things your assistant needs to do while you're gone. Then let your boss, the operations VP, know, through indirect channels, that you're attending the obligatory operations leadership conference and that you'll be gone till Friday.

Awesome! Now grab your travel bag and rush out of the office as fast as your fingers can dial a taxi to the airport. By hurrying off to a conference like this you present yourself as an excellent fit for someone with his or her eye on the higher rungs of the corporate ranks. You're locking in an impression that the rest of your team will remember when the stakes are high and you're set for your next promotion in Week Six. Now, when the cab arrives tell the driver to take you to the airport… and that *"there's an extra $5 bill in it for you if you can get me there in less than eleven minutes."* Nice!

When you arrive at the airport there is more than likely a chance that your flight is delayed, so find the nearest bar, order a whiskey sour or two and then spend any extra time you have by helping out the overworked TSA staff to identify "suspicious" characters as they move through the security check. Remember, the less suspicious a person looks these days, the more likely he or she might be a threat to air-traffic safety. This includes toddlers and even babies! Never, however, participate in a pat-down unless a TSA employee specifically requests your assistance. Also, just because a person looks scary doesn't mean that you should scream and call for help. Think about that aunt or uncle you have. Sure, their looks might have caused the hair on your arms to stand up, but their names would never come up on the national "no-fly" list, would they?

Whatever the case, you're on the InCredidata operations team now, and you have a higher responsibility for those you work with and those in your community. Your willingness to put in some time at the TSA checkpoint demonstrates this new commitment to InCredidata and your country. Once you've spent some time insuring the safety of other travelers, pick up your things, go through security, locate your gate and then find a place to sit down amidst the rows of people waiting to board; then flip open your laptop and make a quick call to your assistant. Ask her to send a file or two over the interweb. It doesn't matter, really, what files they are, just make sure they get to you uncorrupted and that your assistant is busy and doing what assistants should be doing.

When the flight attendant finally calls your row for boarding, enter the plane and find your seat and broadcast a friendly and warm smile as your greet your fellow passengers. While doing this, help an old person to insert his or her bags in the upright compartment. Offer your pillow to someone that looks tired. Once the plane has left the gate make sure that all the seats are in their upright positions, that all electronic devices around you have been turned off and stowed and that no baggage has been left on the floor to clutter up the aisles or rows. If you see any of these things notify the flight attendant immediately by pushing the call button located directly above your head. Quickly point out the offender to the attendant and then return to your close examination of the emergency exits and water landing procedure pamphlet. MAKE CERTAIN EVERYONE IN YOUR ROW IS DOING THE SAME! Then, as the plane taxis to the runway, make sure that the wing flaps have been lowered (…otherwise, your take-off will result in a flaming cataclysm of melting aluminum and plastic), then close your eyes, think of your name with the letters "V" and "P" after it and plan on arriving in Las Vegas rejuvenated and restored!

Hurray! You're on your way to your first corporate conference!

Once you've arrived at Las Vegas and your shuttle bus has shuttled you to your hotel, approach the front desk and insist on receiving an upgrade to a suite—tell them you're from InCredidata and see what kind of reaction you get! After you receive a room assignment and get settled in, call down to room service to send up an couple bottles of wine, some shrimp cocktail, calamari, a chèvre cheese plate, a Caesar salad and an entrée of filet mignon. You deserve it! It's been a long day, and the best thing to do when you're away on business is to eat and drink the things you would normally eat and drink were you at home! Before your dinner arrives, help yourself to the free drinks and snacks provided in the mini bar and, once finished with your dinner, wind down by watching a little pay-per view TV. Don't worry. The front desk knows that all of this is on the InCredidata tab!

Once awake the next morning, call your assistant to check in on how things are going back at base camp and then call a cab to take you to the biggest conference center in the area. When you arrive at the conference center, quickly find a conference and attend it! At any moment of the day in Las Vegas, there is a conference going on, and you can bet your bottom dollar that almost all of these conferences are geared toward some boring and uninspiring topic such as team building or leadership training, or something involving self-empowerment—in other words, an abundance of useless, windy blather and nothing you don't already know. Suffer through this morning session and when lunch rolls around gather a crew of fellow bored-out-of-their-skull attendees and make for the Strip! This gives you a good six hours to blow all your cash on gambling, booze, wedding arrangements, an Elvis impersonator and divorce proceedings! When you make it back to your hotel on Friday morning, gather your things and settle up with the front desk. If they give you any problem with your bill, simply have them transfer the balance to the InCredidata corporate account. If they still have a problem with this, have them call your assistant at InCredidata and have her verify your claim. If this still doesn't work, at last resort, pull out a credit card and pay the bill. But be sure to save the receipt! In two weeks, once you're VP, you can deduct every penny of it with your new VP corporate credit card!

Back at InCredidata, pay a quick visit to your assistant to get the lowdown on stuff that happened when you were gone. Remember, though, you're not stopping by the office to do any work. You're there to make an impression! The more haggard and hung-over you appear—the more you smell like sex and booze—the more respect (i.e. street cred) you'll get from other team-members when you stumble, that day, through the office halls. If asked by a co-worker how the conference went, roll your eyes and tell him or her that the details are so disgusting and crude that they'll go down in InCredidata history. In the meantime, email your boss with a message stating that you'll need the rest of the day off to meet with a divorce attorney. After that ask your assistant for $20, get some fast food, rent a DVD, head for home and call it a day!

You've Done It!

Congratulations! You've completed Week Four of the *Faking Smart! Six-Week Program!* While Las Vegas might have momentarily taken the metaphoric wind from your sails by draining you of all your strength, you've managed, in one week's time, to portray yourself as chief company negotiator and labor arbiter, you've warmed the hearts of the operations team with a genuine display of humor and comic timing and you've collected a bushel of good water-cooler stories to tell about your crazy conference in Vegas. You're at the top of your A-game, and with each day that passes you are one day closer to reaching the goal we've set out for you: to become a VP in *Six Short Weeks—Guaranteed!* Just as no one knows why the sun rises every morning, so is *Faking Smart!* an enigma that has grasped the imagination of tycoons and business scholars from all walks of life and from every corner of this massive sphere we call Earth. *"We don't know why it works,"* quotes the FSRI, *"It just does! So, let's leave it at that."*

You might feel that with everything you've achieved so far you have earned a well-deserved break from the harried schedule of the six-week program. Not so! You have two weeks left before becoming a VP—two weeks of the most grueling and difficult (*yet easy...!*) challenges to face. As if you were a pilot flying blind at 30,000 feet, we are here to talk you down—to glide your gigantic, heavy metal machine through darkness and fog—to your final approach and abrupt, cinematic conclusion—*your name on a brass nameplate with a "VP" next to it!*

Week 5
ZEN AND THE ART OF FAKING SMART!

EXCELLENT! GIVE YOURSELF A PAT on the back, for you've just made it to Week Five of the *Faking Smart! Six-Week Program*. With only two weeks to go, you've proven all naysayers and dubious doubters wrong by participating and excelling in one of the most famous, globe-imploding job-acceleration methods made exclusively for mass consumption! Your final goal stands only a short distance away—becoming a tried and true corporate VP with all the perks and benefits that come with it—and as you make that stumbling sprint toward the finish line, we're here, dangling that carrot in front of you while poking and prodding you in the rear with the ease of a seasoned cart driver coaxing a sleepy old dray horse home to its hay-strewn stable. You can do it! We know you can. If we didn't think you could make it this far, we never would have written this book!

Avoiding *Faking Smart!* Burnout

At this juncture in the *Faking Smart! Six-Week Program*, you may be saying to yourself: *"Man, how much longer is this six-week program going to take?"* The truth of the matter is, having completed four weeks of the six-week program you wind up with roughly two weeks before you presumably reach the title of VP.

Now, this may sound daunting to some, but the FSRI and KWA want to emphasize that you are much closer to finishing the program than it may, at the moment, appear. Sure, you probably have some gnawing notion that you've been run ragged through the past four weeks. Your family members, alert to the increasing command you have over your work life, may begin to exhibit vertigo as you "float" from one job promotion to the next. Your friends and neighbors, joyful yet wary of your corporate good fortune, may be wondering what, exactly, it is that you do, and that if you can find success at the workplace, why can't they? These stresses and strains may combine to throw a dash of *sour* on what should be considered your sugary ride on the *Faking Smart!* express. *"Don't let it get to you!"* states the FSRI. *"Forge blindly ahead and let us worry about the wreckage you leave behind! And don't forget to send your mother a card on her birthday."*

What we are trying to say here is simple: DON'T BE A *FAKING SMART!* BURNOUT! Not that we think there is any possibility of this occurring, it's just that your goal should be seen as tangible now. By coming this far you've demonstrated that you have what it takes to get what you've always wanted: to become a VP, and to celebrate in this inevitable inevitability!

Statistics Never Lie

Up to this point of the *Faking Smart! Six-Week Program*, we've been relatively conventional when it comes to providing strategies and tactics to help you succeed in our program. In each section of each chapter we've laid out in simple, easy to follow directions how to prepare, execute and complete each *Faking Smart!* task so that, statistically, your rate of success meets or exceeds any and all expectations set by our teams of professional scholars, pundits, lab technicians, dry-wall installers and ranch hands. To be honest, if you've made it this far, according to the FSRI, you have a 100.7845% chance of finishing the entire *Six-Week Program* to become an actual VP in two weeks time! It's true (we were equally baffled by this number), but as we all know, numbers never lie, so, to take a step back, if the number given above is indeed accurate (…and why shouldn't it be?) the chance that you will set this book down, quit your job and join a troupe of traveling puppeteers (*before ever becoming a VP*) is exceedingly small! In other words, if you've made it this far in the *Six-Week Program* there is virtually no likelihood whatsoever of you not becoming a VP!

Frankly, at this point in the six-week program, there is hardly anything to stand in the way of you becoming a VP. You know it. You've got that *Faking Smart!* glow about you and if you close your eyes and imagine it… there you are, sitting comfortably behind a VP's desk with your feet kicked up while you riffle through the previous month's sales figures. Ah, now, that's what we're talking about!

Week Five Rundown

Again, congratulations for making it this far in the *Six-Week Program!* To have achieved this level of success in our program is truly something to be proud of, and Week Five, with its focus on workplace Zen, should help you to summon the external appearance of self-confidence and corporate enlightenment that any low-level corporate executive would bend over backwards to achieve.

In Week Five we begin by instructing you on the art of meditation. Once you've mastered the ability to fine-tune your mental focus, we then guide you through a series of sensory challenges aimed at training your mind to transcend imminent physical danger and pain. Lastly, we lead you through a trial of temptation in one of our most serious and impressive tests yet in the entire *Faking Smart! Six-Week Program*: **The Vow of Silence**.

At the end of the week, after completing your accelerated teachings in the field of workplace Zen, we set your free to do as you please. But don't take a break just yet! Your first day in Week Five begins with a trance-inducing lesson in self-meditation!

Monday: The Sound of One Hand Clapping

We all know that if one focuses on something hard enough, it will come true. Zen masters have known this for eons, and now it's your turn to put this esoteric knowledge to practical use in a modern office environment. That's why today we focus on the discipline of meditation and the secret powers of the mind this practice can unveil when used correctly.

After a heroic previous week, set aside some personal time today and do what needs to be done at your home by telecommuting to work. Telecommuting is a way for an office worker to pretend to be working while avoiding the sleep-inducing routine of actually showing up at the office. When you telecommute you stay right at your own home, sleep late, lie around all day on the couch in your pajamas and enjoy martini lunches if you so desire. Just keep in mind that while telecommuting you are presumed, by your team, to be at work while at home, so don't fail to be "in touch" with your office during the course of the day and shoot off a few emails that show you're engaged and not using this block of unsupervised free time to slack off. Yes, it's true your assistant is at work doing everything in his or her power to hold down the fort. Yes, it's also true that your assistant can probably do whatever it is you regularly do at work. Yes, it's true, your assistant has probably become, throughout the course of the six-week program, better at your position than you... but that's irrelevant right now! What is relevant is that you telecommute today to learn how to meditate and prepare yourself for your final week and final promotion!

So, follow the steps below and squeeze what you can out of this day of opportunity and self-exploration:

- Buy or rent a suitable meditation mat—one that will work well when used for several hours at a time.
- Find a location in your house or apartment where you have a place to stretch out and feel at ease.
- Light several candles.
- Find, set up and ignite an incense stick or pyramid.
- Find your television remote and keep it within arm's reach.

Once you've collected these important wellness components, sit down on your meditation mat, close your eyes and let your environment slowly seep into your inner being. Take a minute or two to do this, then, if you want to, turn on the TV to a channel with something peaceful and calming on it, like a soap opera or a 24-hour shopping network or an aerobics program. Now, close your eyes again and try to focus on something that gives you a sense of wellbeing and peace—a cloud, perhaps, or a high soaring eagle-like bird. But, first, and most importantly, make yourself a hot cup of tea. Chamomile tea is an excellent accessory on your path toward personal enlightenment. First, bring a pot of water to boil, then remove the pot and pour the hot water into a cup where the tea bag is allowed to steep while you return to your floor mat and realign your focus on something that restores an inner sense of calm and direction—like the puppy you had when you were a child. (Not a puppy you saw die, or one that was hit by a car and paralyzed or permanently maimed. This won't help you to focus.) If the puppy or early childhood pet doesn't elicit waves of soothing feelings and warmth, trust and safety, try to concentrate on the image of a flower in the woods—a wild flower, but not one that's poisonous or "threatened". And don't try to think of any flowers that don't fit in with the environment that you're imagining it in... like a dahlia in a frozen

Alaskan winter. That plainly won't work. It's too confusing and the image evokes an uncomfortable sense of cognitive dissonance. Stick to the puppy: that's best... or the cloud.

Okay, get your cup of tea and return to your mat. Now, whatever you do, while maintaining your focus don't be distracted by an urge to check and see if the mailman is coming... unless you are expecting an important package. If you are expecting an important package, wait for that package to arrive before returning to your place of focus. Once you've received the package and the mailman has left, open your package and examine its contents to confirm order accuracy, then leave the extra letters that came with the package and return to your meditation mat, sit down, close your eyes and once again try to return to the place of focus you were working to achieve earlier.

Don't be distracted by thoughts of checking your computer for any incoming email. Then again, you're telecommuting, and perhaps, before you revisit your meditative state, you should take a quick peek to see if any messages have come in from the office. If you do have any unread messages—not junk mail—review the messages quickly and then return to your meditation mat. Please, avoid the urge to check your email every two minutes. It is critical in learning the powers of meditation and inner focus that you don't let your attention wander so frequently. If this urge is overwhelming, however, and you are having trouble focusing on a puppy or a cloud, take a few sips at your tea and see if anything is happening on TV. If you're still not in the mood to enter into a deep, meditative state, try getting up from your mat and then take a quick scan of what you have in your fridge. If you feel you must, take a drink of something—like a swig of milk—or, if you need to, grab a handful of grapes or an apple. Take these to your table—not your mat. (Do not use your meditation mat as a picnic blanket.) After you enjoy a short snack, return to your meditation mat and resume your focusing session. Before you do this, however, run your mouse over your email button to look for any critical messages and then determine whether or not you should send your bank account number and password to an earnest, yet desperate Nigerian doctor who has three million dollars waiting for you simply to help him retrieve a ten million dollar promissory note kept in a New York bank. (Of course, this is a scam, but read through the email anyway, just to make yourself better aware of these kinds of confidence schemes.)

Good work! Can you feel the effects of this meditation session stirring deep thoughts and emotions in your inner being? See, that's what this is all about. Now you know exactly what it's like to have a Zen master's sense of focus and mental harmony! Now, take a few moments to complete this meditation session by repeating a final mantra: *"I'll play my part, by* Faking Smart! *I'll play my part by* Faking Smart! *I'll play my part by* Faking Smart!..." Say this 1001 times (...this is a standard Zen number.) No more—no less. Repeat this phrase exactly 1001 times for this to help you with this week's mental training, and if you lose count start over from the beginning.

Excellent! Good work, you've completed Monday's tasks with flying colors. You have taken the first step towards becoming at peace with your work life. Now, shoot an email to your assistant saying that you're signing off, catch a late matinee of one of those movies you've missed while being stuck in Vegas last week, then get a good night's sleep and prepare for Tuesday's mission—where intense and astonishing physical pain makes you better prepared for the challenges facing you in Week Six!

Tuesday: Strength Through Pain

Everyone knows that Zen masters can withstand excruciating pain by retreating, mentally, into a place that separates thought from physical sensation. Today, to complete this stage of your training, your job is to test that threshold of pain, increase it and then eliminate it entirely from your conscious self to build the mental fortitude needed to succeed in the final week of the program! Below is a list of activities that will guide you in your goal. And yes, there's no telecommuting scheduled for today. Go into work as usual, and while working with whatever it is you are working on, experiment by involving yourself in the following tasks:

- While sitting at your desk, bite at one of your fingernails until you have separated part of your nail (a sliver along the side of the nail) that is still fastened to your cuticle. Then take your teeth and bite down on this hangnail and yank, in opposite directions, your head and hand.
- Create a sculpture using origami—the Japanese art of paper folding— while blindfolded! With the thickest and sharpest paper stock you can find, create an origami cubicle through this traditional Japanese

art form. Using valley folds, mountain folds, in-folds, out-folds and pleats, create a replica cubicle that you will be proud of. This may take hours of concentration, reworking of paper folds, promethean determination and severe, if not life-threatening lacerations (...or paper cuts, in this case.) When finished, take a picture of the cubicle, place it for bid online and then clean the pool of blood from your desk.

- After covering your body with paper cuts, walk over to the break room and see if the coffee pot is full and hot. If it is very hot, take a paper cup or a thin plastic cup and pour yourself a full serving—full to the rim. If the coffee is too hot... so hot that you can't hold on to it any longer, throw a quick gulp of it down your throat before it drops and splashes over your lap and legs. 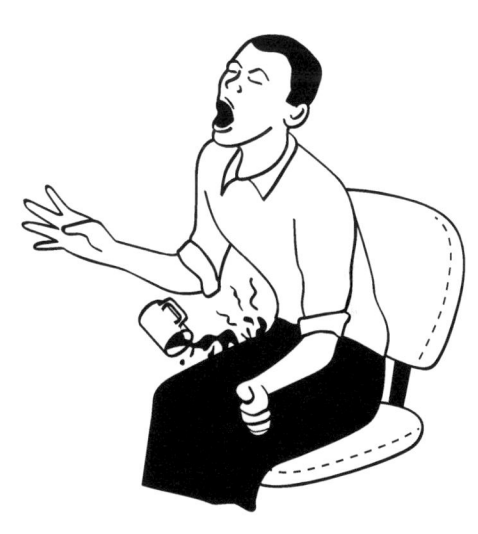
- After scalding yourself with coffee, take a look into the break room fridge and see what you find. Close your eyes and reach as far back as you can, pull out what your fingers come across and then remove the item. With your eyes still closed unwrap the item and begin to eat it. Once you've finished eating half of what you've found, open your eyes and see what you've just swallowed! Can you make out what this was through all the mold and goo? 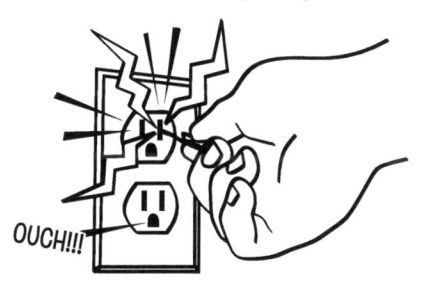
- At your desk, take a paperclip and unbend it so that it becomes an extended piece of steel wire. Now, find the power strip that your computer is plugged into (... or any electrical outlet where an

appliance might be plugged in near you) and insert the end of the paperclip in one of the empty slots. Poke around in this slot as if you were in search of a piece of lint. *Keep your focus!*

- Publicly (or privately) tell a coworker with whom you've been having an affair that he or she is a *"cheap street-hustler with the loose morals of a hedge-fund manager,"*... and prepare for a slap across the face. (Brace—absorb—repeat...) Be sure to thank this person after completion of the exercise by mentioning that you were doing this for character-building purposes and intended neither to offend nor shame.

- While working at your desk, glance up at the ceiling and describe to yourself what you see. Keep looking up. Now try to look further up along the ceiling so that you chair begins to lean further and further back. At some point the feet or wheels on the front of your chair will begin to leave the ground and your legs or feet (propped under your desk) will be the only thing stopping you from falling over. Find this point and stay there for a moment... then close your eyes and release your feet. Now get up and do it again!

- While standing on a stack of phone books and old employee handbooks, change a fluorescent light bulb in a section of your office's suspended ceiling. Stack these books and folders on a mail cart to gain more height!

- Work at your computer monitor with your head tilted sideways at a 45° angle. Do this for two hours straight, then attempt to straighten your neck and back. Now, give your chiropractor a call and set up an appointment for the weekend.

- Beneath your office chair is a floor pad—a durable piece of plastic that protects the carpeting while allowing the wheels on your chair to move freely around the area in front of your desk. Move your chair off this pad for a moment and turn the plastic pad over so that the small spikes used to hold it in place on the carpet are now facing up. Place the chair in front of your desk, sit down, take your shoes off and return to work. After you've been working for a while, get yourself a drink of water... *and ah, yes.* If your feet start bleeding, seek medical attention.

On second thought, given that Zen masters have an incredible aptitude to learn through empathy, in might be best to put your assistant through the above tests. That way you *both* stand to gain the profound and deep knowledge of Zen concentration and mental fortitude! *And heck... it's about time your assistant got something out of the Six-Week Program!*

Wednesday: A Vow of Silence

Before you come into work today you will need to acquire and bring three significant items: first, a small gong; second, a sari or wrap-around robe (if you have neither of these items of clothing, bring a bathrobe); and third, a fully hairless head or skull cap to simulate the shaved baldness of a Buddhist monk. (A swimming cap will do.)

When you arrive at work (there's no telecommuting today), have the robe or wrap covering your body, place the skullcap on your head and hold the gong prominently in your left hand. When you approach your desk, place the gong next to your computer, then log in and begin to work with whatever it is you're working on that day—updating your Facebook account or searching online for a new entertainment system or plasma TV to replace your old one. Sooner or later someone will come up to your and ask you a question like, *"Boy, how 'bout those jokers down at IT? They really did a number on Scott's project."* Your response will be to strike your gong, join your hands and close your eyes. This might go on for several encounters before someone eventually approaches you to ask why you're wearing a skullcap and robe. At this point strike your gong and look in the direction of your assistant. This is to signal your assistant to excuse your peculiar behavior:

> **Your assistant: (your name), *in his/her quest to acquire universal knowledge and enlightenment, has asked that everyone here resist the urge to solicit his/her use of speech for a period of 24 hours. If you wish to ask a question today, please do so by email or inter-office IM. In the meantime, understand that (your name), for the sake of Zen training, presently believes that language corrupts true thought, and s/he will refrain from its use in an effort to pursue clarity and purity of mind. Thank you.***

Good work! Keep it up, and don't forget that your assistant is there to bail you out of any awkward situation. During lunch you'll be happy to learn that the FSRI has allowed for taking a break from the *Vow of Silence* if getting your order right at a fast food drive-through hangs in the balance. After lunch, when you return to work, continue to ignore your coworkers and if you get yourself in a pinch simply strike your gong and have your assistant go through the excuse drill once more. Where you might run into difficulty, however, is if you've been asked to give a presentation on this, the very day of your *Vow of Silence*. If you've been asked to give a presentation on some topic or other regarding some aspect of operations or other, **don't panic!** Remember, a Zen Buddhist never panics, nor does he or she turn down a good old-fashioned challenge!

There are a number of ways of making it through a presentation without the use of speech. The first and easiest, of course, is to sit back and let your assistant do the presentation. This might be the best option. Who knows, you might actually learn something from this—something about how your company operates or where your position fits in the greater scheme of things? The next option is to pre-tape your presentation. If you have a few day's warning about the presentation you need to give this Wednesday, buy a cheap High-Def camera, set up some lights and props and do your power-point presentation on video. When you're due to give the presentation and everyone is all atwitter with excitement about how you're going to pull this off, simply draw down the screen, dim the lights and project your pre-recorded show! If you've received short notice and pre-recording your presentation isn't an option (or your assistant isn't there that day due to illness or some other excuse... or your assistant has become incapacitated due to a sudden attack of illness—*upon hearing that you want him or her to do the presentation*) then charades may be your best way out of this fix! Yes, charades, that time-honored parlor game that consumed countless fun-loving hours in your youth can now be incorporated into saving your skin during your Week Five *Vow of Silence!*

"*First word,*" they call out as you stand before them, index finger raised. Then brush your ear: "*Sounds like...*" they call out with enthusiasm. Then, with one hand, make a slapping motion over your buttocks. "*Spank,*" they exclaim. You nod. Gesture for more... "*Thank*" someone finally shouts. You nod, hold two fingers up. "*Second word,*" someone inserts. You nod and brush your ear. "*Sounds like...*" You lift up your foot and point to your shoe. "*Shoe,*" someone blurts! You nod... gesture for more. "*THANK YOU,*" someone exclaims! You nod! YES! Now you're ready to start getting to the meat of your presentation without breaking your vow. Good luck! And good work!

Your presentation, through the use of charades, may take the entire day to execute, but at least you succeeded without saying a word or breaking your Zen vow. When you get home at the end of the day, you can relax with the knowledge that you did it! The FSRI has decided, too, that if you want to talk at this point you may do so without jeopardizing your Zen training. Feel free to call a friend and tell her about your day at work and get her take on this crazy afternoon. Lastly, if there was someone on your team that didn't get one of your points during your presentation, give him a quick call for the sake of clarification. Now rip off that robe and skullcap, drive downtown to your favorite karaoke bar and let all that bottled-up stress dissolve from your being as you pour everything you have into a poor, atonal, glass-fracturing rendition of Lynyrd Skynyrd's *Free Bird!*

Thursday & Friday

Congratulations! On behalf of everyone here at the FSRI, we wish to extend our thanks to you for your hard work and to announce that we are giving you a break during the last two days of Week Five. That's right, you've earned every minute of it! By following our program to this point you've proven that you have what it takes to make it in corporate America when using the *Faking Smart! Six-Week Program*. You've also proven that we have what it takes to get you this far in our program, *and we'd like to give our selves a bit of recognition here as well!* Sometimes, when you have a program that is so revolutionary and incomprehensible, you have to take a step back and realize just how cool it all is! In a sense, we here at the FSRI are like giant wizards at the controls of an incredible machine, operating levers and buttons from behind a great tapestry to provide you with the level of motivation and direction necessary for you to succeed! That's correct! *We're wizards and you're under our complete control!* That's part of why this program is so easy!

Take it Easy

So, for today, we'd like it if you just took the time to stretch out over the two remaining days and go into work as any normal employee would and get some stuff done! You deserve it! You've gotten this far in the program, so it's about time you were given a moment to collect your thoughts and to do what any normal, non-*Faking Smart!* employee would be doing when he or she executes the duties laid out in his or her job description. When you arrive at work have your assistant get you up to speed on what is going on in the office: what projects are in the pipeline and what deadlines are approaching. Whatever you need to do today at InCredidata (or whatever company it is) go in and get it done! Lend each task before you your full attention and input. Consult with other InCredidata staff working with you and your operations office (...or those that have been working with your assistant) on any crucial project issues that need to be addressed. See that the work you and your team have been conducting is meeting and exceeding the expectations of your superiors. *Yes, it's that simple!* Go in this Thursday and Friday and simply do a good job at work, then, when you meet with your boss next week to make a plea for your final promotion, you'll have a great story and plenty to tell about how well things are going with you and the team!

Get Ready for Monday

The last thing you need to do this week is to prepare for the first day of the following week—Monday. Before you head home for a well-earned relaxing weekend, you'll need to schedule an appointment with your immediate boss—*the boss responsible for promoting you*—for 11 a.m. sharp the following Monday. (Have his or her secretary mark this meeting as *urgent*.) Then go home and prepare your best suit, your best attitude and practice wearing confidence on your sleeve, for your meeting with your boss will determine whether or not you advance right away to the rung on your corporate ladder that we all have been waiting for you to reach: *the rung with the VP written on it!*

Week 6
NAIL THE INTERVIEW-- YOUR PROMOTION TO VP

HURRAY! YOU'VE MADE IT to Week Six, the most important and LAST of your weeks to complete in the exciting and thrilling *Faking Smart! Six-Week-Program!* Everything up to this point, all the training, acquiring of skills, education and moderate expenditure of effort have propelled you to this, the final step in the most revered of any of the *Faking Smart!* six-week programs. When you're *Faking Smart!* you're taking destiny out of your own hands and placing it in a pair of hands that knows exactly what to do with it! That's right. By letting the FSRI lead you on your journey into the future you've placed yourself on a rocket trajectory toward corporate success. Now sit back in your space suit and relax, drink your Tang and let us light the fuse... *and get away!* Next stop, planet VP and the knowledge that, with only minimal interest, a book, some light reading and blind trust in the FSRI, you can do whatever it is we think you should want to be doing!

Your Week-Six Rundown

Unlike the other weeks in the *Faking Smart! Six-Week Program*, this final week may be long or short, depending on your success interviewing for your promotion. You begin the week by implementing the first of the interview strategies given in SECTION A. If you are successful and are promoted to VP in this section then you will be instructed to proceed to SECTION B, whereupon you will be directed to SECTION D, the final section of this chapter. If you are unsuccessful and do not receive a promotion in SECTION A, you will be asked to proceed to SECTION C, whereupon you will be quickly routed on to SECTION D. Whatever the case, chances are good that you wind up at SECTION D. In fact, there is not even the remotest chance of you avoiding SECTION D. There is, however, no chance that you will be directed to SECTION A, then SECTION B and then on to SECTION C. This sequence is impossible! And if all this sounds confusing to you, you are correct! But not to worry, by simply starting at SECTION A you will be provided clear information on how to proceed to the final of these sections: SECTION D.

THE FAKING SMART! SIX-WEEK PROGRAM, AN AWARD-WINNING PROGRAM YOU CAN TRUST!

Did you know that the *Faking Smart! Six-Week Program* is fully accredited by the FSRI and FSIHL? That's right, when you're following the *Faking Smart! Six-Week Program* you can be assured that every detail in the six-week program has been exhaustively reviewed and approved by the hundreds of teams of researchers at the FSRI. Not only has the FSRI given this six-week program the thumbs up, but the faculty at the FSIHL has recently awarded it the coveted *"Best Six-Week Program of the Year"* award for providing its practitioners the highest quality of any six-week program offered by the FSRI! Yes, when you have the backing of the world famous FSRI and FSIHL behind you, you know you're involved in a six-week program that provides results!

SECTION A:
Monday, 11 a.m., Interview I

You have what it takes. You've made it through five full weeks at InCredidata (or whatever company it is). In nearly every week that you've been here you've received a promotion through hard work and dedication to the company. You're sharp, on the ball and everything InCredidata wants in an employee, and you can feel confident that when you go into this interview to ask for a promotion to VP that you will receive it for no other reason than on the merit you've demonstrated. By now your name should be indelible in company history *(...no one has risen so far and so fast)*. Your reputation precedes you. Everything you've done up to this point provides a clear indication that you will give your company the quality and professionalism that is requisite for any executive ready to take on the challenges that lie ahead.

When you enter the office, give a slight bow and a firm handshake to your boss, then state your case. Lay it out as plain as can be: *you want to be a VP and your record should show that every indication points to the fact that you are qualified for the position.* Mention your initial work in the phone center, your work as a manager and finally your stunning rise to the operations team. Be proud of your successes, but not arrogant. Remark on the great people that have been beside you on your rise and the honor you have for being among such a wonderful and talented team—the kind of people that have made InCredidata the company it is today. Remind your interviewer that you have no other ambition than to become a VP and that a decision for or against your promotion should be given by the end of your meeting.

Ask if there are any questions the interviewer may have and answer them with candor.

Stress again the necessity of knowing whether or not you have the promotion by the time your interview comes to a conclusion. If the interviewer asks you why this is important, be honest and state that you don't know. Simply relate the fact that you would like the promotion to VP, and that a resolute answer is what you came here for and all that you seek.

WHEN YOUR INTERVIEW CONCLUDES, ANALYZE AND EVALUATE THE OUTCOME:

1. Did you get the promotion? If so, congratulations! Proceed directly to SECTION B and follow the instructions provided.
2. Were you turned down? If so, don't give up! Remember, we've got your back and have only begun to open the *Faking Smart!* toolbox for getting you your promotion. On your way out of the office be sure to schedule another interview for the same time the following day and continue with the current section.

Tuesday, 11 a.m., Interview II

So, your experience from yesterday has given you a clear indication that merit alone won't get you a VP promotion from this stubborn interviewer. Not to worry. If such is the case, it's time to go at this from a different angle.

When you enter the office this morning for your second interview, go with the same sense of pride and self-worth that you did the previous day. (If you need to brush up on your interview skills, review the *Faking*

Smart! Interview Survival Tips given in the first chapter of this book: "Become Employed!") Today, however, you turn the tables and allow suspicion and uncertainty in your boss's mind to run rampant.

When you sit down in front of your interviewer today, be sure to hum a light melody as you project a wide and contented smile. When your interviewer raises an eyebrow and asks what he or she can do for you (... *things are really busy right now and you should get to the point*) simply let out a long sigh and begin by thanking your interviewer for allowing you to be in the position you are currently occupying. Here is, more or less, how the dialogue will run:

YOU: I just want to tell you how happy I am with my current job. The people I work with are so nice. I love the office vibe. Wow, I mean, if I weren't in the position I'm in now I might have to really challenge myself... you know, go the extra mile to achieve certain goals. But right now, with the harmony and good will down at our department, I don't need to worry about any of that.

INTERVIEWER: Just what are you trying to say? Get to the point.

YOU: I guess what I'm trying to say is... if you were to offer me a VP position right now, I think I might have to turn it down.

INTERVIEWER: Well, you're in luck. You're not getting any promotion from me today.

YOU: And that's why I'm here... to thank you. I know that your job can be hard, and I just wanted to let you know, face to face, that things couldn't be better with our operations team. You should be proud of it. To promote me to VP right now would shake things up, and that's the last thing you'd want to do with a team like ours. Finally, I speak for all of us when I say that you have our respect and admiration... you're easy to get along with, soft when need be, you don't press us and stir things up like other upper-level management steel-drivers try to do. We know that when we come up with an idea, you're game. We know that if there's an excuse to be given for a mess-up, you'll understand. We know you're there for us, and that's what matters.

At this point there are three potential things running through your interviewer's head: first (and most likely), you've touched a nerve. If things are perceived as going so swimmingly down on the operations team, this has to be addressed, and promoting you to VP might just be the thing that needs to be done to shake things up; second, the basic fact that you're so comfortable with your job is a red flag for any seasoned superior, and yanking one out of one's comfort zone is the modus operandi of any honest to goodness higher-up; lastly, you've become a completely annoying employee (you're second nonsensical "meeting" in so many days is enough to drive anyone mad) and the desire to get rid of you may culminate in two very different outcomes.

INTERVIEWER: Well, what if I decided to promote you right now?
YOU: I'd be forced to decline the offer, for my own sake, the sake of the team and for InCredidata (or whatever your company's name is.)
INTERVIEWER: In that case, I've decided. And I'm the decider. Tomorrow you report to me as our newest Junior VP. Take it or leave it.
YOU: On ethical grounds I should decline. On procedural grounds, however, I'm forced to accept. When I joined the InCredidata team it was with the implicit understanding that I follow the direction of my superiors, and that said, I congratulate you on your newest appointee to the position of VP. (Stand, shake your interviewer's hand and take your leave.)

If you haven't figured it out by now, the above scenario is the product of a new type of psychology just now going through its final stages of testing by the FSRI. The above is an example of *flipflop* psychology, a new field of psychology under testing in the Mind and Motivation Labs at the FSRI. Today, with the rapid advancement in application through study at the FSRI, flipflop psychology is applicable in nearly every corporate setting where things need to get done! And using this groundbreaking area of psychology to become a VP is no exception!

WHEN YOUR INTERVIEW CONCLUDES, ANALYZE AND EVALUATE THE OUTCOME:

    1. Did you get the promotion? If so, congratulations! Proceed directly to SECTION B and follow the instructions provided.

    2. Were you turned down? If so, don't lose heart. On your way out of the

office be sure to schedule another interview for the same time the following day and continue with this section.
3. Were you fired? If you were fired, or asked to resign, proceed directly to SECTION C.

Wednesday, 11 a.m., Interview III

Well, so much for that... Even using the pioneering method of *flipflop* psychology wasn't enough to get this hard nut to crack. Never fear... remember, you're *Faking Smart!*, and when you're *Faking Smart!* there's always one more way around an obstacle and there's always a different way to reach a goal! When you enter the office for the interview today go with renewed courage and determination. Repeat these lines to yourself: *"I think I still want to be VP, I think I still want to be VP, I think I still want to be VP."* By repeating this simple phrase over and over again, you might start to believe it yourself! And if you think that you still want to become a VP, the chances of it happening increase exponentially!

When you greet your interviewer present a firm handshake and a nod, then seat yourself. Let out a long sigh and smile and ask your interviewer how things are going with him or her. If a grumble or a growl is emitted, you have your in!

YOU: Thanks for taking the time to meet with me this morning.
INTERVIEWER: What do you want today? You're not getting a promotion.
YOU: Why, what makes you think I'm fishing for a promotion?
INTERVIEWER: This is the third day in a row you've come here requesting an urgent meeting. Two of those days you've wanted a promotion. If I'm correct, you're after a promotion today as well. Well, today you're not getting one. Got it?
YOU: You've made your point. You've made a solid assumption based on empirical evidence and historical reasoning, but I'm here to prove you're wrong.
INTERVIEWER: Please do...
YOU: Allow me to proceed.
INTERVIEWER: As I said, continue...
YOU: Thank you.

INTERVIEWER: You're welcome.

YOU: Listen, we're both here for our own reasons. You, for example, have put in your time. You've worked long and hard to get to where you are. You've sacrificed for this company and you have good cause to argue that you've made it this far by unyielding energy and drive and a desire to succeed at what you do. Am I correct?

INTERVIEWER: *Grrrrrr....*

YOU: As I was saying, you've paid your dues around here. And it's only justified that you receive the honor and accolade that is your due.

INTERVIEWER: Please.

YOU: I, on the other hand, just want to become a VP. That's it. I have no other aspiration.

INTERVIEWER: Your point...?

YOU: Listen, you've worked hard to get to where you are, as I've indicated. Just look around you... you have a nice office, although not quite as nice as some of the other executives'.... But that's beside the point. Your success here has allowed you to live a decent life; a life trimmed with all the material things that help to make you and your family happier and more comfortable: a nice car, albeit not quite as nice as those some of the other higher-ups have; a nice home, although, perhaps, it's in need of a new coat of paint; a nice family, even though you might be struggling at times to make ends meet. From all outward appearances, you've got it made.

INTERVIEWER: Is this leading somewhere...?

YOU: Ha! Please, you do jest! But can I ask you a question, an honest question—a question from one InCredidata employee to another?

INTERVIEWER: Is it possible to decline?

YOU: Have you ever laid awake at night and wondered... have you ever had that gnawing feeling that things just aren't right; that there's something missing in your life and you can't put a finger on it, but it eats and eats away at you until you have to radically divert these darker thoughts by indulgences in, say, an early evening cocktail or two, pain killers or a debilitating fascination with some absurd diversion... like the game of golf, or, perhaps, an obsessive attention toward lawn care?

INTERVIEWER: I don't know. I've never really looked at it that way...?

(Now you've laid your harpoon in deep! From this point on it's all a matter of reeling in the line.)

YOU: I think I might know what can help.

INTERVIEWER: You do?

YOU: Do me a favor. Go over to that window and look out and tell me what you see.

INTERVIEWER: A homeless guy urinating in a trash can.

YOU: No, not that. Look a bit west, and to the south, next to that first lamppost—next to your Toyota.

INTERVIEWER: You mean that black Porsche?

YOU: Bingo.

INTERVIEWER: Is that a 911?

YOU: Targa 4. Right off the lot. Brand spankin' new. 345 horsies. 0-60 in five seconds flat.

INTERVIEWER: My God.

YOU: And it could be yours... *if* you want it bad enough.

INTERVIEWER: (still gazing out the window at the sleek car) In my 20 plus years in the business nobody has ever pulled a stunt like this just to get a promotion to VP. You're either completely crazy or I've underestimated your level of determination.

YOU: (sliding the keys across the desk) Care to take a little drive?

INTERVIEWER: (eyes still fixed on the car) I've got a power lunch with some folks from marketing.

YOU: Cancel it.

INTERVIEWER: You're on.

YOU: Good. I have to get it back to the dealer by 1:30 sharp or I lose my $1000 deposit.

INTERVIEWER: Yeah, I kind of figured there was some sort of catch.
YOU: The idea was solid, though.
INTERVIEWER: No problem... this gives us just enough time to make it out to the interchange and open her up once or twice on one of the on-ramps.
YOU: Ok, but take it easy. I've got this little carsickness thing.
INTERVIEWER: That's why we do this before lunch.
YOU: Brilliant!

WHEN YOUR INTERVIEW CONCLUDES, ANALYZE AND EVALUATE THE OUTCOME:

1. Did you get the promotion? If so, congratulations! Proceed directly to SECTION B and follow the instructions provided.
2. Was your promotion denied? If so, retreat and reorganize *(...and be sure to return the Porsche to the dealer!)* and plan for your next visit. Schedule another interview for the same time the following day and continue with this section.
3. Were you fired? If you were fired, or asked to resign, proceed directly to SECTION C.

Thursday, 11 a.m., Interview IV

If presenting your superior with a Porsche doesn't get you the promotion you're after, the world is a much grimmer place than we here at the FSRI have come to expect, and re-tooling your attack this Thursday is of the highest order of business. The one thing you have going for you today is tenacity... and your interviewer has surely started to take notice of this. Take advantage of this momentum when you greet your superior. Keep the false grins and shallow sincerity—the common currency in professional protocol—to a minimum and try to focus on the task at hand as you lay out an argument for your promotion in which no doctoral logician could find fault!

When you enter the interviewer's office approach the interviewer at once, shake his or her hand and then wait to be offered a seat. After a seat has been offered, sit down and then quickly establish direct and unwavering eye contact with your interviewer.

INTERVIEWER: Nice to see you. It's been a long time…
YOU: I was here just yesterday, don't you remember?
INTERVIEWER: I was joking. Of course I remember.
YOU: (light-hearted laughter)
INTERVIEWER: I suppose you're looking to get a promotion today?
YOU: That's not what I've come for.
INTERVIEWER: Okay. Then why are you here?
YOU: To shed light on an otherwise obscure corner of metaphysics.
INTERVIERER: Oh…?
YOU: To shed light on what we all hold to be true, yet we fail to let this truth serve us in our daily lives.
INTERVIEWER: Ah, you are here to convert me!
YOU: Perhaps…?
INTERVIEWER: Well, it's company policy to keep religion out of the office place. So if you're here to impose your religious beliefs on me, you can leave at once.
YOU: I'm not here to talk about religion.
INTERVIEWER: What, then, are you here to talk about?
YOU: I'm here to talk about choice.
INTERVIEWER: Okaaaaaaaay.
YOU: The choices we all make in our daily lives. If I may,… what did you have for breakfast this morning?
INTERVIEWER: A bagel with cream cheese and a cup of coffee.
YOU: Ah, do you always have a bagel for breakfast?
INTERVIEWER: Interestingly, no. Sometimes I have toast with jam. Sometimes I have the hankering for an egg or two.
YOU: Perfect!
INTERVIEWER: Get to the point…
YOU: You understand that contained within every choice you make, you inadvertently create an alternate universe—a parallel universe, so to speak—where the thread

of your "unmade" choice leads off to unlimited new universes?
INTERVIEWER: Wasn't there a movie about this?
YOU: I think so, but that's unimportant at the moment.
INTERVIEWER: Proceed.
YOU: See, if you had eaten toast with jam this morning an entirely different set of consequences would follow. In fact, had you been offered the choice between toast and jam or a bagel with cream cheese, right now an alternate universe would currently be dealing with that alternate choice and all the sequential ramifications therein.
INTERVIEWER: You're starting to really freak me out. How does this relate to you getting promoted?
YOU: Like I said, I'm not looking to get promoted today.
INTERVIEWER: Then what, by goodness, do you want from me?
YOU: I'm here, simply, to offer you a choice.
INTERVIEWER: A choice, huh?
YOU: Correct. I'm here to offer you a choice. The choice is whether or not you promote me to VP today. Wait. I see you're getting agitated. Hold on. You see, by offering you this choice I've ultimately made your decision irrelevant.
INTERVIEWER: I don't know if it's rage or torpor that's overcoming me...
YOU: It's simple. Are you going to promote me, today, right here and now?
INTERVIEWER: No.
YOU: Great! Thanks!
INTERVIEWER: Why the jubilation?
YOU: Because right now, in an alternate universe, you've just promoted me to VP!
INTERVIEWER: Congratulations!
YOU: Thanks, this means so much to me, you wouldn't know...
INTERVIEWER: Good. I hope you do well in your alternate universe. Now, can you please leave? I have more important things to do right now.
YOU: Of course, of course. But I do have one more question before I go.
INTERVIEWER: And that is...?
YOU: Being I'm a VP in an alternate universe—and I just want to thank you again for promoting me—would it be any trouble, just out of

curiosity, being I'm already a VP in an alternate universe, to promote me to VP in *this* universe? I mean, since I'm already a VP and everything, albeit in an alternate universe?

INTERVIEWER: This smells like you're offering me another choice. True? And no matter what I say here, you'll become a VP again, making it two times I've promoted you today, albeit in alternate universes?

YOU: Ah!, now you're catching on.

INTERVIEWER: Unfortunately for you, that's a risk I can't afford to take. On the other hand, why don't I sidestep your question and pose my own?

YOU: Ok…?

INTERVIWER: So, I'll respond by offering you a choice.

YOU: Uh, oh…

INTERVIEWER: Yep. Would you prefer I fire you on the spot, or would you rather that I permit you to return to your desk and we forget this conversation ever took place?

YOU: Ah, clever… So, either way you've fired me?

INTERVIEWER: Bingo!

WHEN YOUR INTERVIEW CONCLUDES, ANALYZE AND EVALUATE THE OUTCOME:

1. Did you get the promotion? If so, congratulations! Proceed directly to SECTION B and follow the instructions provided.
2. Was your promotion denied? If so, plan for your next visit. Schedule another interview for the same time on Friday and continue with this section.
3. Were you fired? If you were fired, or asked to resign, proceed directly to SECTION C.

Friday, 11 a.m., Interview V

Well, this is it. This is your final day in week six to successfully receive a promotion, so pull yourself together, lay all your cards on the table and let's see what happens. While it may seem like there's a lot of pressure on you to perform today, the reality of the situation is somewhat different. If you haven't noticed by now, a dynamic has begun to form between you and your interviewer—a bond, shall we say—something close to camaraderie, yet still not one of close friendship. Exploit this development in your relationship on your final day. Tear down the curtains, expose the scars and reveal the inner you as you make your final plea.

When you enter the office today, dispense with all the wooden formality customary in professional tête-à-têtes. Avoid the handshake. Sit down before being offered a seat and wear an expression reflecting the gravity of your purpose.

INTERVIEWER: Hey! What a surprise. I wasn't expecting you.

YOU: I've been here every day this week at this exact time. You'd think it was fairly predictable that I show up today.

INTERVIEWER: Ah, you're right, you're right. Can I interest you in a cup of tea? Some coffee perhaps?

YOU: No, thank you.

INTERVIEWER: Oh? What about something stronger? A dram of whiskey, by chance?

YOU: Sorry, not interested, thank you.

INTERVIEWER: How about a cold beer? It is almost noon...? Are you sure? Are you ill?

YOU: No, no. But thank you. I might as well get to the point.

INTERVIEWER: Please do, if that's what you want. I'm listening.

YOU: I don't know if you've realized this by now, but there's been a reason I've been paying visits to you throughout the week.

INTERVIEWER: Really?

YOU: It's true. I've been meeting with you each day with one purpose in mind, and that purpose has been to try to obtain a promotion from you—a promotion to the rank of Vice President here at InCredidata. This has been my singular task and all my will and resolve has been directed in this endeavor.

INTERVIEWER: Oh, well, I'll be darned.

YOU: In the past four days I've tried everything—all reasonable attempts—to persuade you to award me this promotion. I've laid my claim through a demonstration of merit, I've incorporated guile through use of *flipflop* psychology, I've tempted you with bribery (or, at least, the *thought* of bribery...) and lastly I've presented you with the flawless logic of theoretical cosmology... none of which have borne fruit. I remain un-promoted, drained and in despair.

INTERVIEWER: Oh, please. No tears. Please…

YOU: (leaning forward, eyes downcast and moist) At this very moment, I'm going to appeal to your better self and ask you once and for all, will you give me a promotion? Can you find that shred of decency to grant me this one wish? Can you please, find the mercy, find, no, search long and hard for that frayed and desolate thread of dignity that lies somewhere in that beating heart of yours to grant me this base and earnest petition?

INTERVIEWER: Why not schedule a new interview on Monday? Things will be different on Monday.

YOU: I'm sorry, that's impossible.

INTERVIEWER: Impossible? Why impossible?

YOU: Because this is the last day…

INTEVIEWER: The last day?

YOU: This is the last day I can receive a promotion. Monday will be too late.

INTERVIEWER: Will you turn into a pumpkin if you don't receive it?

YOU: I'm sorry, it's the way things are.

INTERVIEWER: I don't understand.

YOU: I'm sorry. Perhaps I've said too much.

INTERVIEWER: (getting up and pacing behind the desk) Maybe it's my turn to come clean now?

YOU: (surprised) Come clean? What do you mean?

INTERVIEWER: I have a confession to make. I couldn't possibly grant you a promotion right now. The reason for this will become apparent shortly, but allow me to say a few words first.

YOU: My ear is yours.

INTERVIEWER: Thank you. (bows, then continues pacing) In my years working at this company, I have never been drawn through such absurdity, such grand and effusive detachment displayed by an employee that a sense of awe and wonder has been restored to my inner being. Never would I have believed that InCredidata would have the proclivity, nay, temerity or foresight, to hire on someone such as yourself. Never would I have guessed that an employee, the likes of you, would have survived two minutes under the oppressive weight of our traditions, our demand for professionalism and our steadfast insistence upon conformity and compliance. (quickly turning in your direction.) You, on the other hand have defied our traditions and rules. You've bent them, folded them, crumpled them up and discarded them as refuse.

YOU: I'm sorry. I did what was asked of me. Nothing more.

INTERVIEWER: (jumping) YES! And that is what is beautiful! Don't you see it? Don't you realize what you've done? Like a captain of a ship lost at sea I've been spying you through my telescope—you, like a tropical oasis emerging on the horizon, growing closer and closer. For six weeks I've observed your progress—your rapid assent. I've watched with glee as you circumvented or destroyed all convention, leapt with joy as you've made a mockery of hierarchy and status, cried tears of amazement as you've taken everything laid out in corporate etiquette, code and canon and stomped on it and degraded it as if it were mere trifle—something odious and small.

YOU: (tears streaming down you cheeks) I'm sorry…

INTERVIEWER: Sorry? Sorry! Why? Don't you see? Listen here… you've done the unthinkable. You've put a spring in my step! You've transformed me! This last week was proof. For the first time in years I've begun to dream again. My sleep has been solid and I awaken refreshed and with vigor. You have bestowed on me the greatest gift of all… the gift of hope and renewed confidence in my ability to reinvent myself—to strike out and be different. I haven't felt this way in years, no, decades, and I have you to thank for it!

YOU: (wiping the tears from your cheeks) Does this mean you'll promote me?

INTERVIEWER: No!

YOU: (sliding to the floor, weeping with grief) Oh, please, please grant me the promotion. Please! I'm begging you. I'm begging you from the bottom of my soul.

INTERVIEWER: Oh, please don't do this. Come on. This is ridiculous.

YOU: Ridiculous… never. If you only understood…

INTERVIEWER: Come on, now. I would promote you… but I can't!

YOU: You can't? I don't understand.

INTERVIEWER: That's right. Even if I wanted to promote you—and I do, I really do—I couldn't.

YOU: Why not?

INTERVIEWER: Because I resigned this morning, before you came in. Effective immediately. I no longer have the authority to promote you, let alone take you out to lunch on the company card.

YOU: Can this really be happening?

INTERVIEWER: It's true. I'm free as of 9:00 a.m. this morning. Today I begin a new chapter in my life, one where I'm in control of my own destiny—one where I make the calls, whether in poverty or in wealth, to do the things I deem necessary and morally sound with regards to my newfound enlightenment and liberty.

YOU: (still on the floor, wiping the remaining tears away) You're a fool.

INTERVIEWER: (coming over to you) Come now, you're not thinking straight. Get a hold of yourself, this spell will pass.

YOU: Oh, it will pass all right. All this work and no promotion... what a joke.

INTERVIEWER: Hey, that's not the InCredidata employee I've come to know and love. Buck up. With your talents you'll be president here in no less than two weeks time. As far as you're concerned, I'm just someone you passed along the way.

YOU: There is no "going on" to become president.

INTERVIEWER: I don't get it.

YOU: This is it. This is the last week of my six-week program. There is no going on... Today is the final interview in the book—the final pages of the last week and last chapter.

INTERVIEWER: What do you mean?

YOU: (reaching into your briefcase to extract a copy of this book) Oh, I'm not crazy... far from it.

INTERVIEWER: (taking the book in hand) "*How to Get Hired, Get Promoted and Become a VP, In Six Short Weeks, Guaranteed.*" (feathering through the pages of the book) Holy mother of... everything, everything you've done is contained in these pages. Everything you've done, to exact detail has been explained and provided to you through this book. Everything...!

YOU: Yep.

INTERVIEWER: What wickedness is this? What foul treachery? What madness!?

YOU: Turn to Week Six, the Friday interview... that's where things get really weird.

INTERVIEWER: (sliding down to the floor beside you, tears welling up as the pages are found) By God...!

YOU: How's that for irony?

INTERVIEWER: (reading further) Irony, you say? This isn't irony. This is something worse?

YOU: Is it? Perhaps this is tragedy?

INTERVIEWER: (a blank stare emerging) Now, to poke out my eyes...

YOU: Get over it. You'll be fine. Why don't you keep the book, though? You might need it.

Be sure to clear the immediate area of sharp implements and take your leave. To finish out the next section of the chapter, go directly to a bookstore and purchase a new copy of this book!

WHEN YOUR INTERVIEW CONCLUDES, ANALYZE AND EVALUATE THE OUTCOME:

1. Well, there is only one outcome at this stage of the six-week program. Proceed immediately to SECTION C and continue.

SECTION B:

On behalf of the FSRI, the FSIHL and the author of this book, we congratulate you on your success! You are now a VP. By taking part in the ***Faking Smart! Six-Week Program*** you have proven that with a little bit of effort, moderate interest and blind devotion to the pseudo-methodologies concocted and ginned up by *Faking Smart!*, becoming a high-ranking low-level executive is within the grasp of any and all who purchase this book and give it a try! Again, we want to congratulate you and wish all the happiness that accompanies your new position as a low-level executive in the corporate world. We knew you could do it! We continually reminded you that you could do it! You did it!

Proceed to SECTION D.

SECTION C:

If you've been directed to this section it is because you've received the disappointing news that you've either been asked to tender your resignation or because you've been relieved of your duties at InCredidata (...or whatever company it was that you worked for). At this point you may be wondering just how this outcome could have happened? You followed all the tactics and strategies to a "T". You put full faith in the *Faking Smart!* methodology. You did everything asked of you, but still fell short when it came to getting that final promotion to VP. *"Just what went wrong,"* you might be asking yourself? Well, the answer to your question may be more complex than it seems. Sometimes, even in a six-week program as thoroughly researched and tested as the *Faking Smart! Six-Week Program*, things can go off course. In the rare—no, exceedingly rare and almost statistically impossible—chance that you weren't awarded a position as VP, we here at the FSRI can only chalk up this shortcoming to publisher misprints or abrupt cultural shifts that were, are and always will be impossible to anticipate and immediately integrate into our program. Believe us when we say: *"It wasn't our fault."* Nor was it yours. It was someone else's fault or "some things'" fault. But learning about these unforeseen circumstances only makes our next printing of this book more effective and better serving for those who dare to jump, unassisted by floatation devices, into the fast moving river that is this program.

With any bad news, however, there is always some good news. You may have been fired or asked to resign at InCredidata (...or whatever), but in our eyes you're a winner just the same! Because you've come so far, so close to earning the title of VP at your company, *we here at the FSRI want to announce that we are officially appointing you to the position of VP in our Special Services Division!*

Congratulations! You are now a VP!

Yes, it's absolutely true! By making it this far in the *Faking Smart! Six-Week Program*, you demonstrated your ability to everyone here at the FSRI that you have what it takes to become a VP in the corporate world! A blank certificate of your official status as a VP in the *Faking Smart!* Special Services Division is provided at the end of this chapter. By simply filling out the form you automatically qualify as an official FSRI VP, with full access to our division coffee room and document copy center! (...although these facilities are currently out of service due to ongoing renovation.)

That's right, you're an official VP! We guaranteed it... you did the rest! Again, congratulations and welcome to the world of big business... a world so big and enormous that you can't do anything but marvel at its existence!

SECTION D:
You're a VP... *now what?*

Whether by promotion through your company or through a default promotion provided by the FSRI, we want to, again, congratulate you on your success. Becoming a VP in the corporate world is no easy task, by any measure... unless you've done it by participating in our *Faking Smart! Six-Week Program!* Yes, by participating in our six-week program you've proven that you can achieve the dreams we think you should be dreaming... **by merely picking up a book and following its instructions!** Once again, we applaud your successful efforts and wish you the best in your new and burgeoning career!

At this point you may think that, at last, you have gained some time to relax—to *kick back, put your feet up and smell the roses,* as they say. But this is the last thing you should be considering. Even though you've finally achieved the title of VP, there are numerous pitfalls and challenges you face by staying with your current company. (For those who've achieved the title of VP in the FSRI's Special Services Division, this might apply to you, as well.)

While you may feel comfortable in the fact that you've reached the goal you set out for at the beginning of this book, the truth is, now that you're a VP, you should begin the process of speedily applying for the position of VP at a different company or firm. This is what is called a "horizontal advancement," and one that will gain you a much better chance of longevity in a newfound company or setting. This "horizontal advancement" is exactly what you need to shed the history you have built at your current place of employment. By shedding this history you avoid any potential legal issues, while at the same time allowing your "soon to be old company" the time to reorganize and reflect on just what might have happened in the last six weeks of its existence. (To tell the truth, nearly every company that has had the fortunate experience of having had a *Faking Smart! Six-Week Program* participant enter their doors has turned to a drastic re-structuring program that has benefitted both personnel *and* Strategic Planning!)

For those of you who have received a default promotion to the FSRI's Special Services Division, we encourage you to apply for a horizontal advancement at other companies as well. While being a VP in the Special Services Division allows you the freedom of being associated with thousands upon thousands of other FSRI Special Services VPs, it may not provide the challenges you may expect as a typical VP in other areas of the corporate world. The FSRI encourages you to STRIKE OUT ON YOUR OWN! and pursue a new job with the full weight of the training you've received at the FSRI behind you! At this point, mentioning the FSRI and the Faking Smart! Six-Week Program becomes an asset rather than a complete hindrance, for the corporate world is slow to assimilate the knowledge of such a cutting-edge, radical program the likes of which you've just completed!

Once again, congratulations on your new position as VP! We knew you could do it! It was just a matter of reading this book and following every step given to you. Now that you've attained the position of VP, feel free to share you knowledge of this six-week program with each and every friend and colleague you can think of, and encourage each of them to buy a copy of this book and let them all know how easy and painless it was to become the highly successful, low-level executive in the corporate world that you've become!

Afterword

Thanks for participating in the *Faking Smart! Six-Week Program!* From all of us at the FSRI and FSIHL, we wish you the best in your career and look forward to hearing more stories of your future successes! **Remember to keep Faking Smart!**

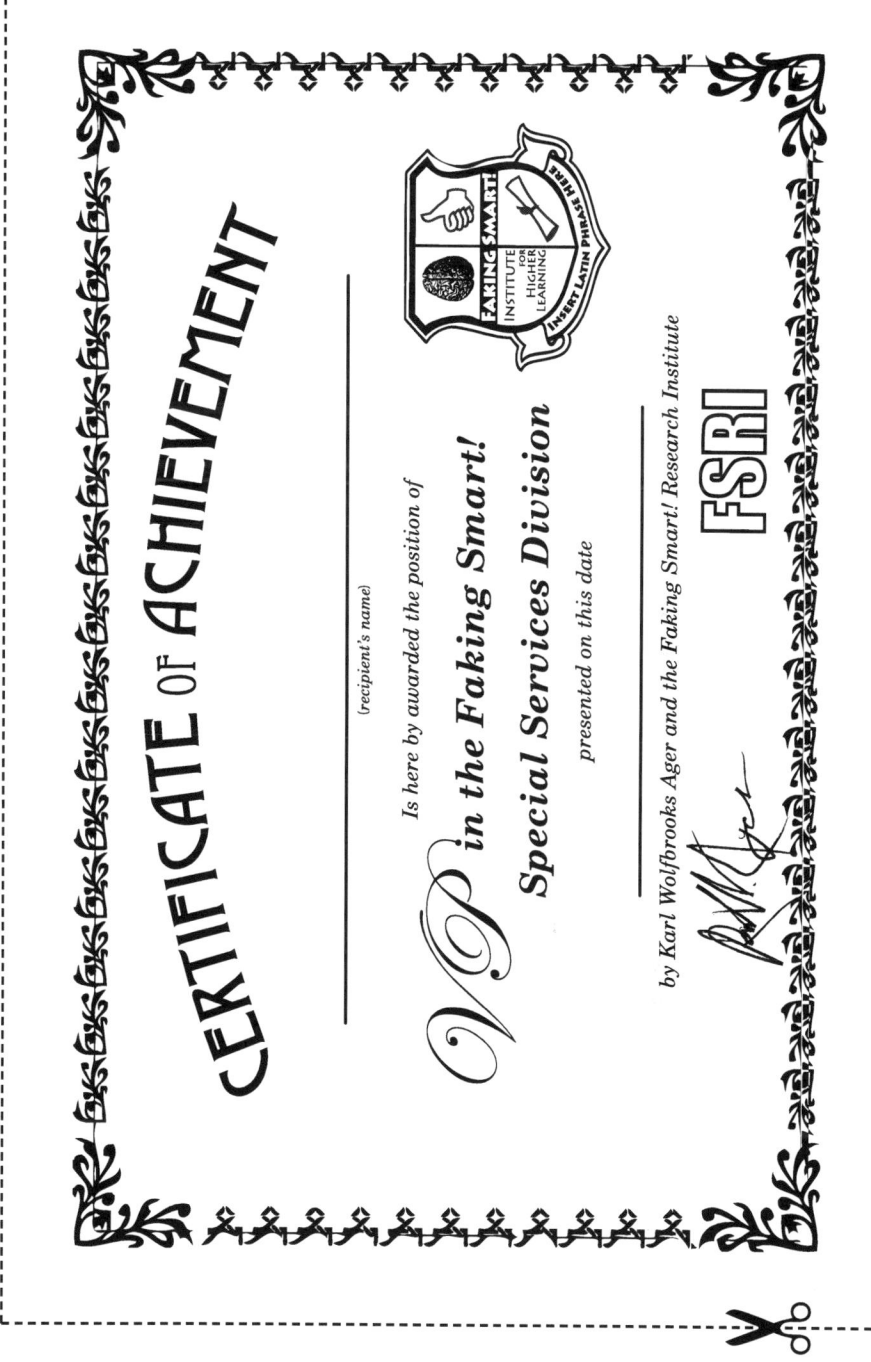

CERTIFICATE OF ACHIEVEMENT

_____
(recipient's name)

Is here by awarded the position of

VP in the Faking Smart! Special Services Division

presented on this date

by Karl Wolfbrooks Ager and the Faking Smart! Research Institute

FSRI

Your official certificate awarding you the position of VP. Just fill it in and you automatically qualify as a VP in the FSRI Special Services Division. Once filled in, simply cut it out and keep it in your wallet or purse as proof of your title.

LEGAL DISCLAIMER:

Any and all complaints filed against the FSRI, the FSIHL or the author of this book should be directed to our Stuttgart division of Legal Affairs at FSRI-Berliner Strasse, 98LO7, Dortmund, Germany. If you fail to hear from us it is due to our current staffing reorganization and location reallocation. We encourage "snail mail" for purpose of documentation, but if you insist, after months of failed attempts through our regular mail address, then please try our current email address: FSRI@fakingsmartinc.org.com. Due to an enormous backlog of correspondence, please allow two to three years for a reply. If your attempt to email us fails, feel free to email us again. We at the FSRI promise you a professional and succinct response.

Made in the USA
Charleston, SC
23 March 2011